YOUR SOCIAL
VISIBILITY BLUEPRINT

A Solopreneur's Guide To
Personal Brand Marketing

JESSICA CAMPOS

ISBN-13: 9798648662469

~

To my amazing family, students, clients, and friends:

You've given me the courage to play a bigger game.
Keep holding my hand! We are in this together!

Jessica Campos

~

Endorsements

Notifications

All	Mentions

 **Mari Smith** 👑 Top Facebook Ma... · 1m ⌄

If You Want To Succeed In Digital Marketing Today You Need To Know What Is UX via @jessicamcampos | We need to be creating experiences that speak to our ideal clients! 🎯

IF YOU WANT TO SUCCEED IN DIGITAL MARKETING TODAY YOU NEED TO KNOW WHAT IS UX

(FREE PDF TO DOWNLOAD)

If You Want To Succeed In Digital Marketing Today You Need To Know...
marketingforgreatness.com

Social Media Examiner #IMS20 ✔ @SMExaminer · Apr 8
Discover 5 creative ways to use the Facebook Messenger platform to improve your customer interactions 😄 bit.ly/2X5VUvA by @jessicamcampos #facebookmarketing #messengermarketing

5 Creative Ways to Use Facebook Messenger for Business
Discover five creative ways to use the Facebook Messenger platform to improve your customer interactions.
🔗 socialmediaexaminer.com

"Jessica Campos has DONE IT -- created the ultimate social media playbook, guide, manual... every title synonymous to 'ultimate guide' applies to her powerhouse of a resource for entrepreneurs. She has put in all the work so we can all sit back, read, and be inspired to create better, more captivating content on our social media profiles. I am impressed by every part of this blueprint. I've written down captions and story ideas I would have never had if I didn't read through her book! Jessica's Social Media Visibility Blueprint is a must-have for everyone using social media to build their brand. Stop wasting time and snag your copy today!"

— Julia McCoy, Entrepreneur,
Author, Founder at The Content Hacker™

"There's a lot that can be learned from Campos' story. For anyone who has had to struggle and has suffered breakdowns of their own, this is where you need to pay attention. Jessica is known as the social media guru and for a reason."

— Ramon Ray, founder of Smart Hustle Media

CONTENTS

INTRODUCTION

If you are jumping into this "new normal" where more things are virtual, and you want to explore social media marketing to grow your business, it can feel like you are trying to catch the fastest train in the world.

Most of my clients tell me: "It feels overwhelming."

Here is what I say in the workshops, coaching calls, and private consultations that I have with solopreneurs: "People buy YOU. If you truly connect with someone who needs your product or services, and make them feel like a human, like you 'get them', you will be able to serve them well."

Social media is no different when it comes to making real connections. As a matter of fact, my book, *The Six Golden Rules of Social Media*, is all about the fundamental principles of making connections online.

Have you ever connected with someone on Facebook or Instagram and, without even talking to them, you feel like you know a lot about them; then you find yourself talking about that person who is still a stranger? That is, essentially, word of mouth marketing! As a business owner, word of mouth marketing should be your number one marketing channel.

Can you see the similarities between social media and word of mouth marketing styles? Other people are your biggest resource in both cases. I think it is fair to say that social media serves as the amplifier to your message since you can reach a broader audience from the convenience of your fingertips.

Current Challenges of Social Media Marketing

There are literally millions of accounts sharing billions of tweets, posts and messages to their followers each day. From major brands, nonprofits, and community organizations to personal accounts, the number of social media accounts continues to grow.

Sometimes cutting through all that noise seems insurmountable.

Successful social media accounts are a result of many factors; However, if there is something that marketers agree on, it is that businesses who are succeeding in social media marketing have a brand, a social media strategy and a plan.

You might be thinking ... "I don't have the budget to hire a team" ... Well, the great news is that if you have a good direction, you can take full control of your social media marketing and do it like a pro yourself.

I have been teaching forensic digital marketing and social media marketing to solopreneurs and marketers for over a decade. From millennials to silver liners, they all have transformed their overwhelm into clarity. And so can you!

I invite you to be aware of the brands that inspire you. Pay close attention to the way they market within their social media platforms. See if you notice their brand personality, the tone of their voice, and the style of their visuals. Also, pay close attention to their audiences' comments and other reactions (likes and shares). This is a simple exercise that can offer you clarity around the brand you would like to build.

Perhaps you already have an idea about the brand that you would like to build. If that is the case, I would ask just to be aware that your biggest asset is YOU.

My vision with this book is to take you on a quick journey where you can get clarity around the brand of YOU; and how to harness the power of word of mouth marketing using social media.

The Social Visibility Blueprint

This book is a vision that was born after realizing that engaging content, pre-written for you, was not currently available. There are thousands of prompts and ideas that you can pull from, but a resource of content to apply to your specific brand was missing from the marketplace. This is where the idea of "plug n' play" content that is crafted specifically for solopreneurs and small business owners was born! With this information, you will be able to input your brand data and customize these engagement-driven pieces of content to help make your social media marketing easier! Who does not love that?

It is easy.

It is user-friendly.

And it does not take a lot of time.

Someone needed to reveal the 1-2-3's of what content truly is in the social media marketing space. A veteran digital marketer with vision, who has a finger on the pulse when it comes to the future of marketing.

Someone needed to take the time and write a "baby food style" (one bite at a time) book so that nonmarketing minded solopreneurs could digest this expert-level knowledge and figure out EXACTLY how to present their products and services using social selling techniques.

Someone needed to draw the map, build the road, and put all the signs up so others are able to navigate easily.

I spent hours on Amazon searching for a complete, simple, and process-based plan. I could not find it! So, what do you do when you find something that does not exist? You create it!

Visibility is a keyword here at *Marketing for Greatness*. This is what we strive to achieve. But why?

Marketing is what you say and how you say it when you want to explain how awesome your product is, and why people should buy it. Marketing alone does not bring you customers.

Your marketing will only generate sales if you are able to convey your message in front of your ideal audience. And that is what visibility is. The best way to increase your chances of gaining customers is to increase your business' visibility. In simple words: you want to get your message in front of as many qualified eyeballs as possible.

Getting your brand in front of the right audience is what we specialize in. All our forensic digital marketing efforts flow into the goal of visibility which ultimately leads to sales. I have developed and published the *Visibility Curriculum* to lead my strategy sessions, the *Visibility Planner* which is an amazing tool for content creators and solopreneurs who want to focus and get more done, and now, this *Visibility Playbook*!

Who is this book for?

This book is for the busy solopreneur who wants to build a personal brand but struggles to find time in their busy schedule. You know, the one who plays Every. Single. Role in the company. Yes, that one! CEO means Chief Everything Officer for you!

It is for the person looking to expand their reach on social media and optimize their digital footprint.

For the solopreneur who wants to cultivate, nourish, and cherish online relationships with their followers. We all have heard the phrase "online best friend."

Your brand can be someone's bestie.

Your brand can be someone's go-to.

And our system will help you get there.

This is for the professional who does not have a large budget to spend on digital marketing.

It is for the professional who wants to grasp the foundations of social media marketing and what it takes to be successful.

Knowledge is power and this book is POWER-PACKED for those who want to learn how to develop their brand persona, and refine how they portray their business online!

Take a moment to consider the following questions:

Do you have the desire to build a strong brand online?

Do you aspire to be known as an industry expert?

Do you want to be a brand that people know, love, and trust?

Are you looking to expand the reach of your business and build more credibility?

Do you want to craft content for your online community that they love and interact with?

Are you interested in gaining more followers?

Do you like it when your community comments and shares your posts?

Do you want to see product and service requests in your social media inboxes?

Yes?

Then this book is for you.

My Story

Well... as I was struggling with writing this part (talking about myself is not that easy), a publication about my story just came up. Great timing!

Here is how Anastasia, the social media marketing manager for the leading automated calendar app vCita, explains "who is Jessica Campos":

Breaking down barriers and overcoming obstacles is all in a day's work for ballsy entrepreneur, Marketing for Greatness guru Jessica Campos. As a young girl, growing up on the idyllic Caribbean island of Puerto Rico, things were far from dreamy. Jessica's childhood was marred with challenges punctuated with tragedy from immense poverty, family drug addiction and ultimately abandonment. One thing that stands out from this time is a young girl's determination and promise to herself to succeed, even without any reference to lean on, no matter the cost or the hard work involved.

To date, with every barrier to success Jessica has encountered, she has managed to overcome everything with her signature self-discipline, hard work, sheer mental toughness and great positive spirit. A self-proclaimed lifelong learner, she still sets herself ambitious goals to achieve.

Mental toughness and great positive spirit are two major things that I want everyone to feel when they are connecting with me; especially mental toughness!

I discovered my calling for amplifying voices when I was 14 years old. I wanted to be a lawyer so I could help people who were in jail. I still remember when I wrote all my due dates in my mirror. Which due dates? All the degrees I needed to get so I could be a lawyer and finally be able to help those in need. This explains why I started college in the summertime of 1994 as a 16 year old girl. I did my high school in two years so I could go to college, get my bachelor's degree as fast as I could, and start law school. Why were prisoners weighing so heavy on my heart? Because I had family members in jail that I started visiting when I was 11 years old and continued to visit until I became an adult.

I do not believe in coincidences. When the mortgage crisis impacted our economy back in 2008, I was a lawyer with six years of experience and had worked my way up from being an employee at a big law firm in San Juan, to going solo and opening my very own law firm, managing over a billion dollars in real estate transactions. What a perfect storm! The real estate industry collapsed and so did my law firm! But my calling for amplifying voices did not.

In Anastasia's words, *"Ask her how she defines herself and she'll say it depends what Jessica we're talking about? There's the single mom and first-generation college graduate and attorney in Puerto Rico. The Jessica who had to fight to reinvent herself after the economic crash that knocked the wind out of her sails back in 2008. Or Jessica's latest avatar, mompreneur of four and extremely successful forensic marketer based in Austin, Texas.*

As a Latina woman, Jessica looked at the ever-widening opportunity gap and, in her inimitable fashion, stared it down all while laughing in the very face of it."

I believe that we cannot let our circumstances define us. We can't. I cannot imagine how my life would have turned out, had I chosen to define my identity as "a criminal's daughter". I am not going to lie, I struggled with this identity for a very long time. I needed to find ways to lift myself from the bottom up. How did I do it? Mental toughness, as Anastasia calls it. It is about attitude. Not winning in life was not an option, period.

When my law firm collapsed, I hit rock bottom. I hated my circumstances so much. But by then I was already a master in mental toughness. In retrospect, my transition from law into marketing was a blessing, but dang, those were some hard days. I was in a season of my life where I had just remarried and was pregnant. I knew I needed to rethink my priorities and dedicate more time to my family. So, I took advantage of the time to really think about my next move.

Can you relate? Did you get into marketing trying to build a new chapter in your life? Are you currently exploring new avenues to generate some income? If you say yes, this means that you're planning your next move. And I'm honored to be part of this process.

I believe that we are always climbing, and success happens when you actually enjoy each part of your climb. Can you do me a favor and search for the song 'The Climb' by Miley Cyrus? Here is a video with the lyrics.

The Climb

I can almost see it
That dream I'm dreaming but
There's a voice inside my head saying
You'll never reach it,
Every step I'm taking,
Every move I make feels
Lost with no direction
My faith is shaking but I
Gotta keep trying
Gotta keep my head held high
There's always gonna be another mountain
I'm always gonna wanna make it move
Always gonna be an uphill battle
Sometimes I'm gonna have to lose
Ain't about how fast I get there
Ain't about what's waiting on the other side
It's the climb
The struggles I'm facing
The chances I'm taking
Sometimes might knock me down but
No I'm not breaking
I may not know it
But these are the moments that
I'm going to remember most yeah
Just got to keep going
And I
I gotta be strong
Just keep pushing on, 'cause
There's always gonna be another…

So yes, I have been climbing... my entire life!

My desire to climb and conquer victories have taken me very far. Honestly, not because I am smarter or special. I am a hard worker and my passion for helping others fuels me on a daily basis.

I believe that we should stay open to reinvent and innovate. When my law firm collapsed, I moved out of Puerto Rico, looking for better opportunities. Little did I know that a P90x infomercial was going to lead me to open the Hispanic market for Beachbody, turning me three years later into an international speaker and trainer, helping entrepreneurs from around the world on how to start a business from home and successfully market on social media.

hey it's Carl i'm here at Beachbody headquarters

Here are some tips to succeed at reinventing:

- ◆ Adopt a "say yes" to opportunities even when they sound intimidating.
- ◆ Find a community where you feel accepted and supported.
- ◆ Never stop expanding your network. This is where social media comes handy!

And... work hard, keeping your eyes on the target to achieve what you want. ANYTHING IS POSSIBLE! You might need to take a U-turn, and that is ok! You will find your path and you will go back to climbing.

I believe that one connection can impact your life and that is why I love word of mouth marketing. I have met celebrities like Chalene Johnson, and Marcus Lemonis from The Profit. I have been called to be on T.V. to inspire small business owners. My "tenacity" story has been shared to inspire many! Meanwhile, I still struggle as a native Hispanic, speaking English with a Spanish accent.

I believe that when people can feel your passion and authenticity, you earn their trust easier and doors open for you. Sometimes, when opportunities come, all you need is to say yes and figure it out later.

When I transitioned from the home industry business to opening my marketing firm in Austin, I knew it was time for me to amplify my own voice. I started my firm with less than $25. Check out the amazing logo I made from an app for less than $5. Bought the domain coachjessicacampos.com and put the website together myself.

Rockstar Social Media School
CoachJessicaCampos.com

I took massive action and invited my network to my very first Academy. About 35 people signed up that month. They did not know this, but that revenue prevented us from being homeless that month. It was a God thing.

Today, coachjessicacampos.com is where I promote my personal brand. We are now a bigger company, MarketingFor-Greatness.com. My company leads one of the most amazing networking groups in Austin! And guess what? They love my accent!

I also believe that building a personal brand is more about action than theory. As you keep open to opportunities, your career evolves, and so does your brand. Had I not acted and decided to network in Austin, I would never have had the platform that I have today. Sometimes, action must be im-perfect action. I was too embarrassed to speak in English. I say "beach" and sounds like "bitch", "sheet" sounds like "shit" ... "focus" sounds like "fuck us". But I did not let my fears stop me. Meanwhile, gurus told me to market only to my Spanish audience.

I believe I am a living testimonial of what a powerful brand, impulsed by social media marketing can do for anyone who is willing to put in the hard work.

What Do You Need to Build a Brand?

Unlike what many people think, your brand is not about your business name, colors, website, and logo. Your brand is your message.

Your message should be able to build a relationship with your users.

One thing that I attribute to my years in the direct sales industry is that I learned how to make friends and win people. I learned how to recruit. How to persuade. I was a recruiting machine!

To this day, I carry over the good things from the industry, such as:

1. Embracing the power of building a community with customers
2. Leading with positivity
3. Promoting parties and fun activities!
4. Marketing a culture and a value system, more than anything else

Collaborate, Co-create, But Never
COMPETE

MarketingForGreatness.com

The more I focus on helping others, and detach myself from the financial outcome, the less I have to think about marketing myself. That is part of the ripple effect of brand building.

What's Next for Jessica Campos- Marketing for Greatness?

Whatever is next for me, personally! I take my business with me. We are in constant evolution! It's the climb.

I am currently experiencing many joyful moments! This month alone, I was in Austin Woman Magazine, in their Woman To Watch segment! It feels like all the pieces are coming together. I am even writing a book about my personal journey! Born to Be YOUnicorn.

I have evolved my brand to claim the niche of forensic marketing. I am passionate about education so I educate for Fortune 500 companies. Holding the title of author and educator for Social Media Examiner is one of my biggest proud moments. This is something that four years ago I would NEVER even think of as a possibility.

AUTHOR: **Jessica Campos**

How to Build Facebook Custom Audiences for Special Ad Category Groups

 by JESSICA CAMPOS / FEBRUARY 11, 2020

Are you trying to run ads to people for services that Facebook restricts due to possible discrimination? Have restrictions on audience targeting impacted your ability to reach leads and customers?

I have a burning desire to keep speaking for organizations who want a marketing strategist and educator. I do not know where my marketing strategies and teachings will take me, but I promise you something: my calling for amplifying voices is strong and clear.

Now let's dive in.

PART 1:

The Essentials of Social Media Marketing

How, Exactly, Does Social Media Marketing Work?

Social media works great as a word of mouth activator.

Word of mouth marketing impression results in five times more sales than a paid media impression, and people are 90% more likely to trust and buy from a brand recommended by a friend. Motivated future buyers will ask their friends for recommendations before making an important purchasing decision.

Think about this for a moment: when you purchased a car, for example, you did not just go to the dealership, take a test drive, and immediately bought the car. Perhaps you did, but let's be honest; by the time you stepped into the dealership, you had done some research. Your inspiration for that specific make and model came from somewhere!

Future buyers inquire and research. If you happen to be a service provider, your future buyers will stalk you on social media for a while before reaching out to you.

In social media, users will come to your account motivated to find out more about you because:

- A friend referred them and showed them your social media channel.
- They saw advice you offered in the comments of a public forum such as a group or public feed, and your profile picture and comment attracted them.
- Your profile came as a suggested friend and they checked out, got a great first impression, and decided to reach out.

Other than these reasons, in order to get people wanting to work with you, you need to find connections and treat them the same way as you do a new connection that you meet offline. It is about adding value and cultivating those relationships. Social media interactions are no different than real-life encounters.

When you activate the power of social media marketing, you do not know when those friends of friends are scrolling through your page to consider contacting you. At some point, you will wake up with new pending messages, leads, and even clients!

The question becomes, not if, but when. That is why you need to be ready for those motivated users who can be future buyers.

Do Social Media Generate Sales?

The purchasing process has endured remarkable change. Just a decade ago, digital marketing was about having a website and entering some keywords for SEO. That was it! The golden era of Internet Marketing!

Facebook, Twitter, Instagram, YouTube, Pinterest and TikTok were not a thing.

Do not get me wrong, website and SEO are in fact table stakes for a competent e-commerce presence. What has changed, however, is that people now spend significant portions of their time on and within social networks built around their interests and relationships. As a result, the buying process has moved from one driven largely by a desire to find something, to one that is more based on customers coming across things within the experience they have already created for themselves.

In a nutshell, intent and discovery are woven more closely together. The challenge is to be there with those customers when it counts. The solution is social selling.

What Is Social Selling?

Buying and selling have always been social activities. Think about your first sale ever. Perhaps, some of you spirited entrepreneurs were only seven years old or so!

Mine was in first grade and I had to knock on doors asking for donations for the Red Cross. I still remember the sound of the soda can where we had all the coins. My pitch was: "Mrs. ____, would you like to cooperate with the Red Cross?"

This was an ongoing campaign that our school participated in often. At the age of 11, I had won the top producer award! I created a bake sale, in addition to knocking on doors and asking for a favor! I guess we can say I was born for marketing and sales.

I am pretty sure you have some memories too!

But what is social selling? Is it about being social and selling to people? The answer is NO. Social selling is a buzzword that carries a great deal of misconception.

Some people associate social selling with generating sales directly from social media channels, which is NOT accurate.

A social selling method is predicated on the fact that consumers "socialize" with others as part of their decision-making process. This means that instead of selling directly to a consumer, convincing them about their needs and featuring the benefits of your products or services, you ignite those social conversations so consumers can make their decisions.

Here's how Kissmetrics defines social selling, at a glance:

- Endorsing a customer on LinkedIn.
- Running LinkedIn searches for outbound targets.
- Liking a client's Facebook post.
- Sharing the company's latest blog post on Twitter, LinkedIn, Facebook and Instagram.
- Studying prospects on LinkedIn and Twitter before a meeting.
- Following key accounts on Twitter. Retweeting a client.

Social selling was not born as a result of social media.

Before our lives were lit by thousands of screens full of stories and boomerang videos, people asked others they knew and trusted for buying advice. Social media has further ignited the power of social selling, which is why generating revenue through social media must rank high as one of your goals.

Who Should Have A Social Selling Strategy?

Social selling via social media and word of mouth marketing complement each other very well. Incorporating word of mouth marketing (WOMM) into social media is key for increasing leads by 50% or more. For example, Instagram reported that one in five Instagram stories leads to a direct message.

In other words, when you create content on Instagram, 20% of the time it will lead to an opportunity to start a conversation with a potential customer.

You do not even have to do any selling.

In fact, studies show that 92% of people take family and friends' recommendations and word-of-mouth over traditional marketing — This is powerful!

Social Selling Is For Every Business Model

In marketing and sales, you will often hear people talk about business to business (B2B) or business to consumer (B2C). But you rarely hear that marketing is about connecting with humans.

At the core of every marketing, advertising, or communications campaign, there is the same basic human desire: to connect. And while it can be easy to forget, B2B's are often also B2C's. The reality is, we tend to find that what is good for the B2C is also good for the B2B.

Historically, more traditional B2B marketing has focused on connecting companies to one another. B2B marketing often focuses on the rational attributes that make a company great. And while it is important to have content marketing that educates peers, there is a missed opportunity if you are not also taking advantage of the double coverage in the power of establishing real connections.

Creating dual messaging that appeals to both B2B and B2C audiences is one of the great untapped opportunities for brands to take their marketing to the next level. Creating a story that translates across channels and audiences while transcending time creates vast brand awareness, which helps businesses maintain forward progress. And this approach is not just a logical next step. It is measurable on the backend of your marketing efforts too.

If your goal is to become visible to your ideal audience, instead of thinking about them as the role they have in their company, you need to see them as humans first. Regardless of your business model, your marketing will be about getting visibility in front of individuals, so you can ignite connections.

People do business with people they like, trust, and believe in. Social selling empowers conversations and by doing that, you can build trust and engage with future consumers/partners. For this reason, for both marketing models (B2B and B2C) social selling is a fit!

Ingredients Of A Successful Social Selling Strategy

When I teach social selling in my workshops, LinkedIn Workshops in particular, I explain my Hamburger Method. It is a multi-ingredient formula that needs to be applied as a whole. Just like when you eat a hamburger (or vegan burger!). You cannot just eat cheese and say it is a burger.

For a social selling strategy to be effective all the ingredients must be matched together.

6 C's To Design Your Social Selling Strategy

Let's cover each in detail.

1) Consultative Selling Approach

Consultative selling is an approach that focuses on creating value and trust with a prospect and exploring their needs before offering a solution.

A great way to explain consultative selling is by saying what it is not. Consultative selling is the opposite of transactional selling or direct selling.

In a consultative selling model, the salesperson's or solopreneur's first objective is building a relationship; their second is providing the best product or service.

Do not make the mistake of approaching people, requesting a connection, and pitching them your products or services. That is not what relationship marketing is about.

Being consultative helps you in two important ways:

1. By maintaining a focus on building relationships and connection with the client, respecting where they are, and maintaining a genuine sense of care and concern for them, it creates a positive buying experience for the client and fosters an ongoing relationship built on trust.

Relationships = Trust:

2. Once trust is built, they gain needed information to deeply understand the client's needs, identify the right solution, and tailor what they say about products to ensure relevance and impact.

Solopreneurs can adopt a consultative selling model. Adding that personal touch can increase conversions.

If you take a step back though, consultative selling makes sense. It helps sales team members or solopreneurs qualify prospects faster while tailoring a product solution to match their needs. Not to mention reducing customer churn in the long run.

2) Content

Notice that I wrote content and not content marketing. Content marketing is also a buzzword. This puts entrepreneurs at risk of receiving wrong advice; Therefore, getting wrong results.

Your content is a derivative of your communication. Your communication gets shared via your message. A clear message is needed before putting a content marketing plan in place. This is an ingredient that, in my opinion, many entrepreneurs miss.

Perhaps you heard that you need a blog and share information so you can get people to find you on Google. While that can be true, blogging will be considered a key factor of your social selling strategy if the content is relevant to your target audience. In particular, decision-makers.

According to the statistics collected from Kapost, the website conversion rate is six times higher for those who have adopted content marketing strategy than those who have not, and there is a whopping 75% increase in marketing qualified leads through content only.

Content is not just about writing. If you want to captivate users and seduce them to buy from you, you will also need a strategy. A process with tools to ignite conversations and leads, and a tracking system to measure performance.

And, of course, as part of your content strategy, you need to consider how to generate content that ignites social interactions. That is where you can sell without having sales conversations!

3) Culture

Culture is an unmissable ingredient of our recipe for success, especially if you are looking to play a bigger game. But what exactly is culture?

Culture is essentially a combination of the values and behaviors instilled in a company's workplace. Some people call it corporate or organizational culture.

While it is being referred to as an element needed to attract good talent, it also helps to attract great customers.

At the end of the day, I believe that when we align ourselves with people that share the same values, magic happens.

No matter the size of your team, in order to attain success using a social selling/consultative selling approach, everyone needs to be on board with the following behaviors that reflect your values:

◆ Lead with education
◆ Represent a culture of respect
◆ Being a positive influence in their community

But why is all this relevant to sales? Because sales happen when people have positive conversations about your services or your products. And when we say people, we refer to conversations that happen both, offline and in social media.

---

4) Connections

So, your new sales approach has so far 1) Consultative selling approach, 2) Content, 3) Culture. With these three, it is time to put the theory in practice. Connecting with your audience.

Connecting with individuals can seem like "common sense"; However, you will be surprised by how many sales efforts fail at this level.

When we say you need to have connections as part of your new social selling approach, we are not saying: "go ahead and spam 50 people a day". Believe it or not, this is what plenty of professionals do on LinkedIn as their "LinkedIn marketing".

People will want to connect with you as much as they connect with your products.

How can you make your brand desirable, so people want to connect with you? It is easy! Building customer relationships is all about delivering value to your followers.

If you can provide helpful, informative, or even entertaining content, people will want to connect with you. Unfortunately, there are still many brands out there that take the "what's in it for me?" approach to social.

If you are ready to flip the script, start by listening to your audience. If you are starting, your audience is your circle of influence. Start there! Ask questions!

5) Conversations

Imagine you and I just met at a doctor's office and you ask me: "Would you like to lose ten pounds?". Would that be appropriate? Absolutely not.

The same rule goes for online conversations. This is common sense, right? It does not seem to be a common practice for some social media users.

Now that you are turning your social sales game on, you need to get used to some "data waste management".

You commit to only engaging in sound conversations and at the same time, you become more selective with the data that comes to you. Do not be afraid to delete people, remove them from your connections, or even block them.

Did you know that LinkedIn takes into consideration the quality of your connections? Yes. It is not fair, but it is the truth. The more quality connections you have, the more visibility your profile will get.

You might be wondering, but how much time do I need to do all of this? To prepare content, connect with people with authenticity, and ignite real conversations.

I am not going to lie here. A social sales strategy is commonly rejected by sales teams because of the amount of time it takes. The best practice is to outsource parts of the implementation of this strategy such as:

- Content research
- Content writing
- Content distribution
- Preliminary connections

Outsourcing these tasks will give you more time to practice social selling offline.

- Networking events
- Speaking and workshops

♦   Attend to conventions

Now that you have a social selling mindset, your activities will be more strategic. Do not just go out to socialize. Apply social selling instead.

6) Conversions

The last C of our 6 C's of social selling is conversions.

So many people want a high conversion rate without re-searching, defining what is a conversion, and testing their conversion sources. Do not be one of those people.

Like any marketing activity, if you cannot measure it, you cannot predict it.

Here are some of the metrics you should watch to make sure your strategy is in good health:

♦   Monitor web traffic with Google Analytics.
♦   Monitor the organic search appearances with Google Search Console.
♦   Add a clear call to action on your website, including your blogs

Typically, until you reach about 5,000-6,000 web visitors per month consistently, your main focus should be increasing web traffic. After you hit the benchmark (5,000) then you can focus on increasing conversion rates.

For now, implement your social selling strategy and clearly define your conversion points and strategies.

Points of Conversions in Facebook & Instagram

- ♦ Messenger messages. Opening rates as high as 80-90% and click-through rates significantly higher than email.

- ♦ Private groups – building community among your devoted fans, prospects and customers.

- ♦ Stories (and potentially other ephemeral/micro-content) – Zuckerberg has also said in the past that 'stories are the future'.

What Results Should You Expect Immediately from Social Selling?

As soon as you establish your sales strategy and have real social conversations, you should experience an increase in engagement on social media, an increase in the number of people reached, and new connection requests from new people. This should happen within your first 48 hours. Yes, it is that effective.

Now that you know about social selling, it is time to discuss social media marketing, but not the boring way!

Social Media Marketing Is No Different than Socializing in Person

When you meet someone, you try to get to know the person and the person tries to get to know you. We do not necessarily try to sell someone we just met our products or services. We simply connect. These are the principles to apply to your social media and not just in your personal life.

When you start making real connections, you leave an indelible mark on your audience. At this point, people will research you. People will want to know more about you, what you do, your story, and who you are connected to. This is because *First Impressions Last*.

After listening to what you have to say, your background and story along with what you are currently doing will be the core interest of your audience. This is because people want to be able to identify with you or be inspired and motivated. This is why branding is very important. You must represent your message well.

When a prospect visits your social media handles, what they see must enhance and coincide with your message.

If you have not read my book, The 6 Golden Rules of Social Media, I highly recommend it! It is a short book that I wrote a few years ago, explaining step-by-step how I used social media marketing to generate leads in my golden days in direct sales.

Write it down!

The 6 Golden Rules of Social Media Recap

The 6 Golden Rules of Social Media

Golden Rule 1: Make Real Connections

Golden Rule 2: It's Not About YOU

Golden Rule 3: Be Personal, but Not Private

Golden Rule 4: Offer Value, Not a Sale

Golden Rule 5: Be a Story Teller

Golden Rule 6: Engage and Follow Up to Get the

Return on Your Investment

JESSICA CAMPOS

JESSICA CAMPOS

It seems like, regardless of which philosophy we follow, connecting with humans is the common denominator.

Human connection is an energy exchange between people who are paying attention to one another. Well, you cannot really touch someone from your social media channels, but you can certainly use words and build that opportunity to initiate a conversation.

Human connection has the power to inspire change and build trust.

What Is Social Connection Then?

When researchers refer to the concept of "social connection", they mean the feeling that you belong to a group and generally feel close to other people. Scientific evidence strongly suggests that this is a core psychological need essential to feeling satisfied with your life.

Emma Seppala of the Stanford Center for Compassion and Altruism Research and Education, and author of the 2016 book *The Happiness Track* wrote: "People who feel more connected to others have lower levels of anxiety and depression." Moreover, studies show they also have higher self-esteem, greater empathy for others, are more trusting and cooperative; Therefore, others are more open to trusting and cooperating with them.

Brené Brown, a professor at the University of Houston Graduate College of Social Work who specializes in social connection, said in an interview that "A deep sense of love and belonging is an irresistible need of all people. We are biologically, cognitively, physically and spiritually wired to love, to be loved and to belong. When those needs are not met, we do not function as we are meant to." We may think we want money, power, fame, beauty, eternal youth, or a new car, but at the root of most of these desires is a need to belong, to be accepted, to connect with others and to be loved.

How to Connect in a Disconnected World?

As of 2019, the average daily social media usage worldwide amounted to 144 minutes per day. While there are some predictions that users are becoming more mindful about social media usage, we do not foresee this number getting much lower.

Our Brains Are Suffering the Effects of the Switch Cost

The impact of social media and smartphone usage in our attention span is real.

According to a study by Microsoft from 2015, the average human being now has an attention span of eight seconds. This is a sharp decrease from the average attention span of 12 seconds in the year 2000. This is called **The Goldfish Effect**.

In addition to our attention spans getting shorter, when it comes to social media, there is enough evidence to support the effect in our brains.

Your phone sitting there, constantly lighting up throughout the day creates this pattern in the brain scientists call "switch cost."

It essentially means when there is an interruption, such as a notification, we switch our attention away from the task; then must return afterward, which is costly in terms of brain power as well as time.

"We think it interrupts our efficiency with our brains by about 40%", Scott Bea, a psychologist at Cleveland Clinic told CBS. "Our nose is always getting off the grindstone, then we have to reorient ourselves."

This study is very interesting. The team recruited 19 young people with a mean age of 15 and a half, who were diagnosed with smartphone addiction, and a control group containing people of the same age and gender. The addicted group was given nine weeks of cognitive behavioral therapy, modified from a treatment program for gaming addiction.

They were also asked questions about the severity of their addiction, and how it affected their daily routines, social life, productivity, sleep and feelings.

"The higher the score, the more severe the addiction," said Hyung Suk Seo, a professor of neuroradiology at Korea University in Seoul, and lead author of the study.

Addicted teenagers also had significantly higher scores in depression, anxiety, insomnia and impulsivity, he added.

Constantly waiting for the next notification can put you on the edge. Meaning that when it comes through, your body releases cortisol, causing your heart rate to jump. Being away from your phone can also cause some people to have feelings of panic, known as phone separation anxiety.

I do not think that this information surprises you.

Do you feel that it is hard to keep up with notifications?

Have you ever felt overwhelmed?

Do you feel like it is impossible to catch up with everyone's updates?

I get it. I have been using social media to market my business since 2009. Those were the good times! But things have changed, especially the speed of communications! Gone are the days when you could answer an email in 48 hours. I had a client who got offended because I told her that I was not going to answer emails on Saturdays. And actually, she was right. It was my fault. I needed to clarify that weekends were not **working days**. But, wait... Shouldn't that be the norm? Never assume.

When I became aware of the challenges that social media brings to users, I began to study other disciplines like UX (user experience), content writing, UX writing, and information architecture (IA).

The more I integrated all these disciplines, the more I saw the need for a shift.

On a curious note, my book, *The 6 Golden Rules of Social Media* published in September 2016, is now more relevant than it was before. The book covers the essentials of social media marketing.

Social Media Strategy

A social media marketing strategy is a summary of everything you plan to do and hope to achieve on social media. It guides your actions and lets you know whether you are succeeding or failing. Every post, reply, like and comment should serve a purpose.

The more specific your strategy is, the more effective the execution will be.

How to Get Started

A social media strategy starts with establishing a clear goal; However, if you have never done social media marketing, you might set up unrealistic goals.

Your ultimate goal is to find passionate leads from your social media marketing. Leads are the heart of your business, period.

Finding Leads on Social Media Is Still a Wide-Open Path

You might think that the race to find motivated leads is very competitive. The good news is, there is a need for authors, experts and masters with real wisdom!

Gone are the days when you can write a blog, call yourself an expert, and get clients from self-proclaimed victories. Don't get me wrong, I do not think you need to have a Ph.D. to be recognized as an expert, but you certainly need natural talents and practice.

The 10,000 Hours Rule to Mastery

I get to consult with professionals who want to develop digital products very often. They typically want one of two things: to have a plan to transition from their current job or scale their current business.

My initial questions are around their mastery and accolades and very often I tell them: "You have a very good problem. Your brain is worth a fortune and all I need to do is to develop your brand voice around your existing expertise."

Do we need 10,000 hours to acquire a skill? According to Gladwell, yes; However, this statement was based on research suggesting that practice is the essence of genius. Since this theory assumed that practice was "the magic number of greatness", regardless of a person's natural aptitude, evidence suggests that the 10,000 hours alone are not enough. In other words, to be a master, one needs knowledge, experience and natural talents.

What if you do not have a mastery? Do you have to wait until you can claim that you are an expert? Absolutely not.

This is where a mentor comes handy. The mentor-protégé relationship is the most efficient and productive form of learning. The right mentors know where to focus your attention and how to challenge you. Their knowledge and experience become yours. They provide immediate and realistic feedback on your work so you can improve more rapidly.

Discovering Your Calling

I feel like the concept of branding can be very confusing, and I want to put those fears to rest.

Jeff Bezos is widely quoted saying: "Your brand is what other people say about you when you are not in the room". But the truth is, effective branding means there are no "other people" in the process of brand communication. If your branding is rooted in authenticity and everyone (yes, everyone! Aim high!).

When I teach about branding, I realize that my students don't have a question about what branding is, which makes sense since we have been exposed to brands since we were born. Their real challenge is about who they are and how will people perceive them.

The first move toward mastery is always inward— learning who you really are and reconnecting with that innate force. Knowing it with clarity, you will find your way to the proper career path and everything else will fall into place. It is never too late to start this process.

Balancing Personal and Work Life- What Do I Share?

The other aspect where I find that my clients struggle the most is how to keep their personal life separate from their business life. It is almost like they have a life at work and another life outside of work.

What if you could just live your life in fulfillment and your work would fit into it, not the other way around? When your work is something connected deeply to who you are, not a separate compartment in your life, you develop a sense of your vocation.

Does that spark joy? I hope so! I can 100% guarantee that you will not regret your decision to play a much bigger game. You might not know all the steps, but that is ok.

The Mastery Gap

Here is a fact: everybody starts from zero. This is another "panic zone" that I find very often, especially in individuals with a mastery who struggle with technology.

Embracing your apprentice status makes you human. Being transparent with your clients will get them trusting in you more. According to a study, 73 percent of consumers say they are willing to pay more for a product that promises total transparency.

I was asked at an interview "what is the one thing you wish you would do differently when you started your business?" That was such a great question! I told them "I wish I had claimed my true worth since day one." I cannot go back in time and change it, but I certainly can advise new business owners to never make the same mistake.

Your apprentice status does not give your clients a discounted price.

The 7 P's of Your Wondrous Social Media Marketing Strategy

1- Planning

To plan your visibility is like playing a game of chess; it requires focus, a strategy, and the right move at the right time.

A very simplistic way to cover this first part of your strategy is by asking yourself: where are you and what are your next benchmarks? *Your answers will help you set attainable goals.*

- Do you need to build a personal brand? Yes? Then, you are in **development mode**. Your initial benchmark is getting this done. Get crystal clear about how to market the brand of YOU.

- Do you have a personal brand but want to grow your audience? You are in **growth mode**. Your first benchmark is to increase your sphere of influence. Depending on where you start, your milestone should be 5x or 10x your number of personal contacts.

- Did you grow your social media channels, but there are no conversations? You are in **optimization mode**. Your benchmarks are associated with your lead generation and conversions.

Having a clear vision of where you are and where you want to be allows you to make strategic moves.

2- Presence

Let's face it; evading social media presence is not an option – You want to target an audience, you have to get them where they are, and it's 'online.'

Regardless of which of the 3 phases discussed above: development, growth, and optimization, your social media strategy needs to consider your online presence.

- If you are in **development mode**, then you need to build your presence. Putting yourself on social media is more complicated than it seems. Don't overthink it. Work within your strengths. Instead of thinking you need to be everywhere to be successful, work to master one platform at a time.

- If you are in **growth mode**, your social media marketing strategy needs to consider how to generate more followers, engagement, reach, and reviews. This is all part of your online presence.

- If you are in **optimization mode**, your social media marketing strategy should consider ways to incorporate search engine marketing, search engine optimization and paid traffic.

Statistics show that it is a make or break in a split of a second when it comes to online visitors establishing an opinion of your brand. Therefore, you must be smart about how to make your online presence look appealing, reliable, and legit for the targeted audience.

3- People

Third in line but probably the most important P of them all – People. In other words, your targeted audience. Always remember consumers put brands on the map, not companies. I cannot emphasize enough how vital it is for you to base and build a reputation and persona of your product around your clientele.

Who is the kind of people who will be passionate about connecting with you? Do not just think about your product. Before people get interested in buying your products or services, they need to buy you. Your job is to market YOU:

- ◆ Your hobbies
- ◆ Your story
- ◆ Your accolades
- ◆ Your background
- ◆ Places
- ◆ Culture

Anything that can help you engage in conversations with people with common interests.

4- Product

Your social media marketing strategy should pick the key features and benefits, along with key pain points that your products or services solve.

A powerful way to market yourself in a new field is by using your story. People buy your why.

Your branding and your social media strategy should consider YOU as the product. Think of ways to get people to relate and connect with you first.

5- Placement

I would strongly suggest for you to address some factors while formulating your ideal social media placement strategy. You must know where your audience hangs out the most. There are several ways to find this out, such as asking yourself which social media you would visit if you were to find a new doctor or a new attorney? Or a more direct approach is to email your connections for their opinion.

You must also consider other factors like the time and resources that you have.

Can you get leads on Instagram? Yes, you can.

Tips to Get Leads From Instagram

- Learn Instagram for Business so you can understand the best practices to get engagement from potential clients.
- Instagram transactions are mostly B2C, so do not expect a big crowd of people to be excited about your real estate tips. This is normal for B2B content.
- Qualify your leads by having direct conversations with people.
- Use stories to communicate with users.
- Create a landing page for your Instagram so that people can learn more about you and your services on their own time. This is the famous link in your bio.
- A lead generation system works as long as you are willing to put the time and effort to network with people. Just like in real life!

6- Performance

When it comes to strategizing around performance, there are two leading roles: setting up your basic trackers, and designing a series of events to go back and analyze your performance.

Remember the three phases we discussed above: development, growth, and optimization.

If you are just starting to develop your brand, set up a tracking system so you can pay attention to the following:

Impressions - how many times the platform distributed your content

Reach- how many people saw your content

Engagement- how many people showed a reaction

If you are in growth, then you will add another tier of elements to track. For example, if you are running Facebook and Instagram Ads, you will pay attention to:

- ◆ Clicks to your website or landing page
- ◆ Cost per ads results
- ◆ Ads performance

For those in the *optimization phase*, your social media needs a more robust content marketing strategy. Pay attention to:

- ◆ Your call to actions on your landing page
- ◆ Your content marketing campaigns
- ◆ Your email marketing performance

As long as you consider performance as part of your social media marketing strategy, even when you are just using Facebook Insights and Instagram Insights, you are good to go.

7- Processes

Your wondrous social media strategy is almost done! Since you have created all these projects to market your business on social media, now it is time to discuss your processes.

So, what is a process anyway? A process is a series of actions or steps taken to achieve a particular end.

Critical processes to consider:

- Content writing process
- Reputation marketing process
- Social media management process
- Lead generation and lead management
- Sales process

Each process has steps. And each step can be worked either on a daily or weekly basis. That is why you need to be strategic! Or else it will make you feel overwhelmed, and you will throw the towel in just a few weeks.

The Ultimate Secret to Get Followers

Ten years ago, in those dark days before the advent of streaming services, DVD box sets and the occasional TV marathon were the only ways to get your binge-watching fix. These days though, streaming services like Netflix, Hulu, and Amazon Prime are making binge-watching—watching two or more (sometimes much, much more) episodes of a single series in quick succession—an acceptable and fast-growing practice.

For many viewers, binge-watching gives us an escape from the day-to-day grind. Entertainment has always offered a way to escape from the pressures of daily life, and binge-watching is no exception.

Cultural anthropologist Grant McCracken, who coordinated with Netflix on the above survey, sees a correlation between the rise in binge-watching habits and our desire to escape a never-ending sea of bite-sized social media posts and YouTube videos. He explains:

"TV viewers are no longer zoning out to forget about their day. They are tuning in, on their own schedule, to a different world. Getting immersed in multiple episodes or even multiple seasons of a show over a few weeks is a new kind of escapism that is especially welcomed today."

So, as it turns out, it is not the show we are craving; instead, it's the feeling of pleasure we get from watching episode after episode. "You experience a pseudo-addiction to the show," Dr. Carr explains, "because you develop cravings for dopamine...Your body does not discriminate against pleasure. It can become addicted to any activity or substance that consistently produces dopamine." Source: Wistia.com.

It turns out that users will change a habit just so they can binge-watch content they love.

Nowadays, creating content for social media is not just one post. A major shift is happening in our digital behavior, especially after our latest global pandemic, COVID-19.

According to Forbes, COVID-19 Pushed up Internet use 70% and streaming more than 12%. What about social media channels? Instagram alone reported an increase of 2 million users from February. The highest difference between men and women occurs within people aged 35 to 44, where women lead by 3.3 million in February and by 4.1 million in March. It accounts for 800,000 more active female Instagram users in this age group.

The surge of new content consumers creates a gap for those new users who are now seeing social media content and are trying to adapt.

Marketers need to pivot, in order to meet the needs of those new users' requirements.

Your goal is not to have followers, but to create the binge-watching effect.

Social Media and UX Trends We Cannot Ignore

In the modern digital economy, "UX" is the latest buzzword. Organizations everywhere are looking for creative thinkers capable of transforming their businesses through imaginative interfaces and beautiful user experiences.

But What Is UX Anyway?

User experience is a person's emotions and attitudes about using a particular product, system, or service.

If you have recently heard about this and want to know a perspective from a marketing educator who is not an engineer, you will enjoy reading this!

UX is user experience. And you are interacting with it every single minute that you are in front of your phone or computer. You just don't know the word or the meaning just yet.

After hundreds of hours of research, I have curated the best stats and facts that will enlighten you about user experience and why it matters today more than ever, especially in social media.

UX Overview – Strategy

By definition, a UX strategy is the plan and approach for a digital product. UX strategies help businesses translate their intended user experience to every touchpoint where people interact with or experience their products or services.

Brands have been implementing user experience strategies for a while now. My favorite example is Amazon.

I found an article in Quartz that shows a screenshot of Amazon's home page circa 1995 (see below). In today's digital everything world, this website will not make the cut.

Welcome to Amazon.com Books!

One million titles, consistently low prices.

(If you explore just one thing, make it our personal notification service. We think it's very cool!)

SPOTLIGHT! -- AUGUST 16TH
These are the books we love, offered at Amazon.com low prices. The spotlight moves EVERY day so please come often.

ONE MILLION TITLES
Search Amazon.com's million title catalog by author, subject, title, keyword, and more... Or take a look at the books we recommend in over 20 categories... Check out our customer reviews and the award winners from the Hugo and Nebula to the Pulitzer and Nobel... and bestsellers are 30% off the publishers list...

EYES & EDITORS, A PERSONAL NOTIFICATION SERVICE
Like to know when that book you want comes out in paperback or when your favorite author releases a new title? Eyes, our tireless, automated search agent, will send you mail. Meanwhile, our human editors are busy previewing galleys and reading advance reviews. They can let you know when especially wonderful works are published in particular genres or subject areas. Come in, meet Eyes, and have it all explained.

YOUR ACCOUNT
Check the status of your orders or change the email address and password you have on file with us. Please note that you do not need an account to use the store. The first time you place an order, you will be given the opportunity to create an account.

ROI of UX

Here is what is interesting about this dinosaur-looking website!

At the time, of course, the discipline of user experience design for the web was in its infancy, just like Amazon itself. But as Amazon grew from fledgling bookseller start-up to the world's largest internet-based retailer, it thought about the

ROI of UX and continued to invest heavily in providing the best possible user experience for its customers.

Why? Because the company realized there was a direct connection between the quality of the user experience and the bottom line. As founder Jeff Bezos noted back in 2000 about those early days:

"In our first year, we didn't spend a single dollar on advertising... the best dollars spent are those we use to improve the customer experience."

Hmmmmm ... I think we are onto something!

Amazon reasoned that if they could improve the customer experience to the point where they could easily find what they wanted and buy it with a couple of mouse clicks, then sales would grow. So, they did! Take a look at Amazon's path to $1 trillion in revenue.

What can we learn about UX from the Amazon example?

The primary takeaway from my perspective is that it clearly illustrates the direct relationship between the quality and sophistication of the user experience and the bottom line. Any good design obviously needs to weigh the specific business objectives of an application against the user experience, so it is not surprising that there is a strong link between the two.

This was the case with Amazon as it launched and continually refined its e-commerce website, and it is the case today for companies developing software applications for consumers and businesses.

An outstanding user experience can have a positive, quantifiable impact on the business in several ways, whether it is saving money, selling more products, or increasing customer loyalty and satisfaction.

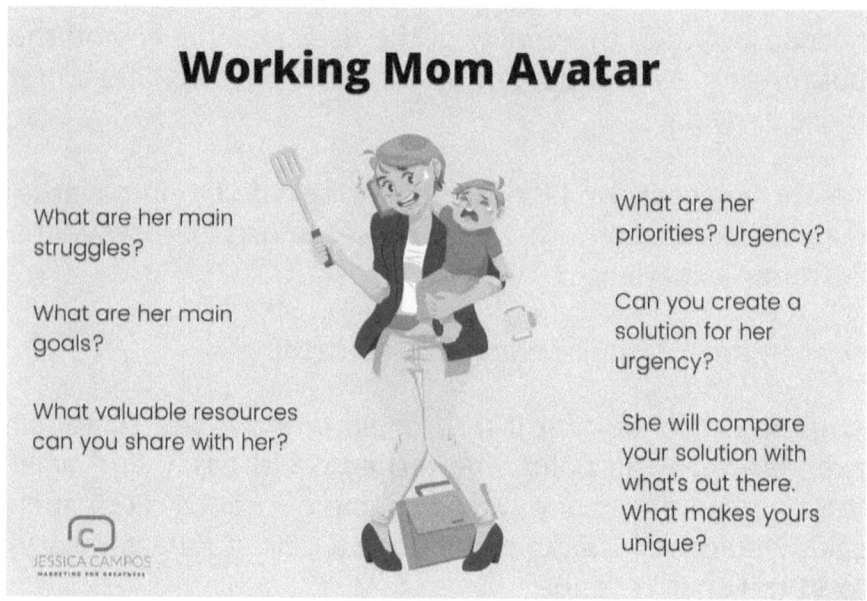

Traditional marketing has always covered the buyer profile or avatar analysis since visibility can only be achieved when your message reaches your ideal customer. The opposite is just noise.

While the avatar profile is not a new exercise, modern digital marketing incorporates UX best practices to consider not only their demographics and purchasing intent, but also their digital behavior.

Some examples of digital behavior that social media marketers should consider:

- ◆ Which social platforms do users engage more in?
- ◆ Preferences based on generation.

- What kind of customer service channel do they prefer? Email? Chat? Bots? Phone?
- What kind of visual design would they prefer?
- Do they consume videos? What length?
- Do they like stories?
- How do they use social media?

Are your people on social media?

Absolutely, yes.

Social media was once associated with only the younger generations, but now, all generations use social media as part of their daily routines. More than 80% of every generation uses social media at least once per day.

The key is to understand that your targeted generation will have usability preferences. Brands who honor their users' wishes and make it easy for them to get what they want, the way they want it, will win the path to visibility.

I have shared with my clients how our marketing team identified an opportunity to generate leads without using email marketing. Our emails were getting dry. Low opening rates. Low click rates. So, I decided to test a new approach. I told my team I wanted to "unmarket" our business.

Why would you possibly "unmarket" your marketing firm business? It makes no sense.

Well, it worked!

- We stopped offering free webinars for lead generation.
- We stopped Facebook ads to generate clicks to our website.

- ♦ We stopped all automated campaigns.
- ♦ Deleted all the freebies and downloadable forms.

Then, decided to try the unmarket route:

- ♦ Hosted local events in Austin.
- ♦ Opened an invitation-only community.
- ♦ Tied our community to exclusive interests.
- ♦ Elevated our Google marketing game.
- ♦ Quadrupled our content marketing.
- ♦ Designed an Instagram-based social media strategy to connect with new people and for the community to connect with existing connections.

This plan was never done looking for quick results. We noticed our website traffic increasing over time.

In just 12 months our website traffic went from shy 40ish users a month to over 15,000 users per month, ORGANIC. And we are still working on optimizing this number to get in the 100,000's.

Our clients have increased by 70% from our *unmarketing* tactics. In fact, this book is part of the mission to educate and give our users nothing but the best content.

I invite you to take a look at your approach with digital marketing. It should serve as the amplifier of your connections but never replace the person to person approach.

True story ... I live in a small-trendy town in the suburbs of Austin. It is a small town, so we have about 4 places where you can get your nails done. I go to the one by HEB since it is very convenient. So, as I'm usually asking questions when I am getting services done, I asked the owner: "Do you guys advertise here?" He said: "No, I don't need to do any marketing. All my customers come from referrals. My marketing is just to do a good job for my clients". Kenny is his name. His clients know him, and you can tell he is very passionate about his nail salon.

Wouldn't it be great to get to that point like Kenny where you don't need to do marketing?

Now that we want to give users what they want, the way they want it, let's talk about content! The infamous 'C-word' that makes solopreneurs cringe; especially when they do not consider themselves good writers. Sounds familiar? Keep reading!

What About UX Writing?

Hey... UX writing is not about writing the best poems. In fact, it could be almost the opposite.

UX writing is the practice of crafting UI copy that guides users within a product and helps them interact with it. Wait, but what is UI copy? It sounds like a different language but let me explain. "UI" in UI design stands for "user interface". The user interface is the graphical layout of an application.

Experts who analyze how users behave online, meaning, where they click, what makes them initiate comments, likes, etc., have created guidelines. This is why websites have headlines to identify specific parts of the pages. Those have a reason. It is not random. In fact, usability tests have reflected that users read in F shape. We are not getting into details here, but I just want you to know that amplifying your message is not just about who can write pretty words.

Interesting UX Writing Findings from Steve Krug

The very famous UX educator Steve Krug, in his book, *Don't Make Me Think*, covers the fundamental principles about UX writing.

- A lot of happy talk is the kind of self-congratulatory promotional writing that you find in badly written brochures. Unlike good promotional copy, it conveys no useful information, and it focuses on saying how great we are, as opposed to delineating what makes us great. Instruction must die.
- Get rid of half the words on each page, then get rid of half of what is left.
- Your primary role should be to share what you know, not to tell people how things should be done.

If there is something you need to remember is that *less* is more.

A Minimalist Approach to Social Media

Now that we are leading your online marketing strategy from the UX perspective, it is totally ok to minimize the number of platforms you use to promote your brand.

Maybe go from seven accounts to three or four quality channels that align with the vision of your brand. Focus on the health of your brand by growing customer relationships and contributing to a conversation. Just think of the kind of value this could add to your business.

The hard part of pursuing a minimalist social media strategy is selecting which channels are the ones that will bring you the most value. I think it's also hard because of FOMO (fear of missing out). I see this a lot!

Again, lead your decision thinking of the kind of experience this could add to your users. And for sure, start with your website!

PART 2:

A Guide to Personal Branding

Your Brand Board- 1 Page Branding Blueprint

Before we craft the amazing content writing plan to market your brand, we need to take three steps back and discuss the brand of YOU.

I promised you practical marketing. So, let me show you where I want to take you, so you have an idea of what you're about to do, in order to create the brand of YOU.

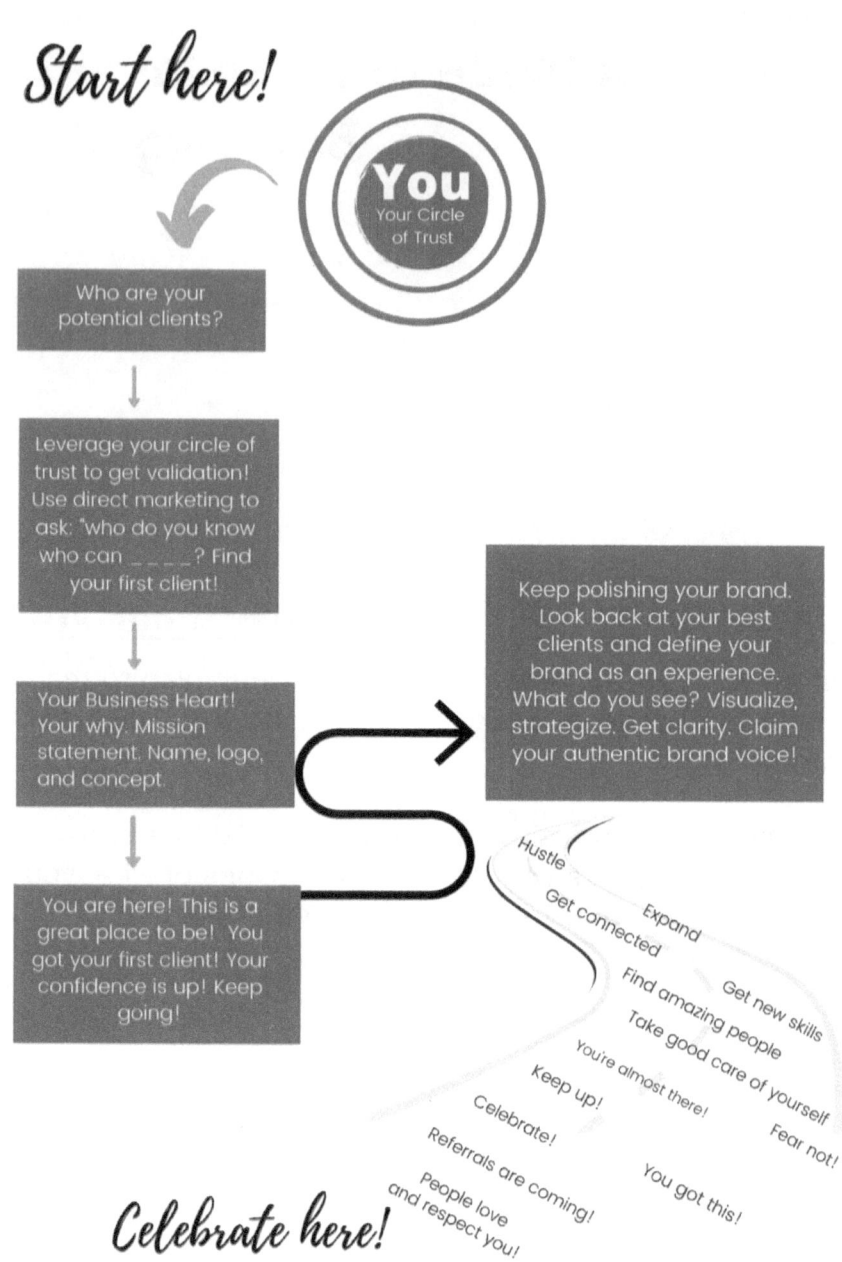

Start here!

You
Your Circle
of Trust

Who are your
potential clients?

Leverage your circle of
trust to get validation!
Use direct marketing to
ask: "who do you know
who can _ _ _ _? Find
your first client!

Your Business Heart!
Your why. Mission
statement. Name, logo,
and concept.

You are here! This is a
great place to be! You
got your first client! Your
confidence is up! Keep
going!

Keep polishing your brand.
Look back at your best
clients and define your
brand as an experience.
What do you see? Visualize,
strategize. Get clarity. Claim
your authentic brand voice!

Hustle
Get connected
Expand
Find amazing people
Get new skills
Take good care of yourself
You're almost there!
Keep up!
Fear not!
Celebrate!
Referrals are coming!
You got this!
People love
and respect you!

Celebrate here!

Are YOU a Brand?

Yes, you are a brand.

If you are a business owner, no matter if it is small or big, you crave one thing: brand loyalty. A strong brand loyalty transfers into repeated customers who buy your products or services, regardless of changes in price or convenience.

Brand loyalty isn't about likes and followers. You can't deposit likes in your banking account! So, we need to make sure your marketing & sales efforts translate into steady cash flow and profit, of course. Make no mistake, your focus needs to be on building a strong brand, followed by developing brand loyalty.

Does that make sense?

If so, experiential marketing should be part of your next marketing strategy. What is experiential marketing and how can you start running some experiential marketing campaigns? Keep reading because I am covering it all.

What Is Considered a Strong Brand?

Amazon CEO, Jeff Bezos, defined the brand very simply as "what people say about you when you're not in the room."

Seth Godin, a popular entrepreneur and blogger, gives a longer definition:

"A brand is the set of expectations, memories, stories, and relationships that, taken together, account for a consumer's decision to choose one product or service over another. If the consumer (whether a business, buyer, voter, or donor) doesn't pay a premium, make a selection, or spread the word, then no brand value exists for that consumer."

Your brand gets represented through in pretty much everything that your business does on a regular basis, including the four following areas:

♦ Visual Brand Identity, such as your logo, website and color scheme

♦ Brand Voice, such as your blog posts, mission statement, social content and website copy

♦ Brand Values, such as the types of causes your company supports

♦ Brand Personality, such as your company's culture and customer service philosophy

The path to building a strong brand does not need to be complicated. Many marketers make the mistake of narrowing their efforts to customer acquisition.

If this has been your approach, you're doing exactly what your competitor is doing.

How can you stand out?

The way you overcome this obstacle is simple. ***Build something money or products can't get you: a genuine connection with your customers, or community.***

A strong brand is a result of connection and community. You can have the most beautiful website or write the perfect sales page, but you will not build a strong brand or reach your revenue goals effortlessly until you build a strong connection and community.

Kendra Scott – A Strong Brand Example

When I think of a strong brand, I like to think about Kendra Scott, for example. If you know of her jewelry, chances are you know about her story. How she went from a $500 project in the spare bedroom of her home to a billion-dollar fashion brand loved globally.

If you have visited one of her stores, chances are that you have a memorable experience.

And just in case you still have not heard about Kendra, let me give you some context. She is one of the top America's richest self-made women and she ranked higher than Taylor Swift, Beyoncé, Donna Karan and Diane Von Furstenberg. It is amazing when you think that beading classes and $500 was all she needed to start a business.

There is a reason why Kendra Scott's locations are flourishing in the middle of the "retailpocalypse". She has been able to create a connection and a strong community, using experiential marketing.

During a workshop about branding to a group of women in business, I asked participants "why do you think that Kendra Scott's brand is so successful?". They told me things like ... "because she has been very active in her local community" ... "because she gives back" ... "because she empowers women" ...

What do you notice about their responses?

The things they remembered about Kendra Scott were all related to the things they have *seen* her *doing*. They didn't say anything about her prices, quality of products, or where the jewelry is designed. And I will add that each had a different perception of Kendra Scott's brand. I would like you to read this again!

Do not be obsessed with finding your name or your title, please! You might not know exactly the name that describes the services that you do or how do you help people and that is ok. Let them perceive your value!

What holds you back from creating the brand of YOU?

From my experience, from coaching hundreds of entrepreneurs on how to develop their personal brand, I can tell you that clarity is usually their missing ingredient.

They have the idea of what they want. They know that they are capable of achieving big things. They just don't know how to do it, and when they see from the outside how others have done it, they get intimidated. They compare themselves with others... and those ideas are never born.

If you are reading this today, I want to put an end to your doubt. So, let's get to work.

Where to Start Defining the Brand of YOU?

Since we are here to be practical, I do not want to get into any lecturing. My two cents here will be that you try to do the best you can to take imperfect action. Please! Ask! Ask your circle of trust and try to see if they will be able to help you.

Sometimes we do more for others than what we do for ourselves. Keep this in mind. ... Make some bold moves.

Who will you call today to ASK? Examples of the questions you can ask:

"Hi _____, can I ask you for a favor? I'm working on my business idea and want to run some thoughts by you..."

"Hi _____, are you still working at _____? You're so great at _____ and I am wondering if you can take a look at a business project I am working on and give me your honest opinion about the _____."

Notice that I am talking about your circle of trust. Some experts say that there are five circles of trust: self, family and personal relationships, organization, market and society.

For practical purposes, from your potential circles of trust, ideally, you want to discuss your business idea with someone who has been where you want to be. Someone who can bring that experience.

Do not just take opinions from people who will always say yes to you. If you cannot find advice from people with experience in your immediate circle of trust, then ask for recommendations!

Lastly, if you want to get started and want to reduce your risks to fail, consider hiring a mentor that can hold your hand through this process. I can tell you from experience, the very first time I hired a mentor, I had been working for three years, trying so hard to build an online business. I waited way too long!

Once I started working with my mentor, in 6 months I achieved what I had not achieved in 3 years. Mentors are there to help you shorten the path to grow your business. And I am not saying this to get you working with me. I am the first to tell you that I work with mentors all the time. You can't read a label from the inside.

Signing Up Your Very First Client

Let me just tell you, signing up your very first client is all you need to validate your business idea. For this reason, you just want to achieve this goal as fast as you can.

From experience as a top achiever in direct sales, igniting 7 figures in team volume, I learned that the key to building momentum in your business is to "force" your success story as fast as you can.

Success loves speed!

When someone tells you YES, they are not saying yes to your shiny logo, beautiful website, or flashy business cards. They say yes to YOU.

What makes people buy from you?

Spoiler alert! My book, **Why People Don't Buy From You**, has hundreds of reasons why you might not be closing your sale. You will love this read!

Most entrepreneurs don't consider themselves good in sales. If you are one of them, then, to get your first client, we first need to shift your sales paradigms.

Your Sales Paradigms

Bob Proctor, master in the Law of Attraction says: "Paradigms are a multitude of habits that guide every move you make. They affect the way you eat, the way you walk, even the way you talk. They govern your communication, your work habits, your successes and your failures."

For the most part, your paradigms did not originate with you. They are the accumulated inheritance of other people's habits, opinions, and belief systems. Yet they remain the guiding force in YOUR life.

Negative and faulty paradigms are why 90-something percent of the population keeps getting the same results, year in and year out.

When I teach our *Visibility Method*, I start asking questions such as:

- Why did you start your business?
- Was there a pivotal moment in your life that ignited this business?
- How long have you been working in your industry?
- What is your favorite part of what you do?
- What areas of your business do you think you could do better if other people were working on them?

It is very possible that you do not see yourself as a salesperson. I have news for you! You are a salesperson. The main difference is in the perception that you have about salespeople.

There are plenty of sales paradigms that might be blocking you from your success story. Listen carefully to your mind when those limited beliefs come.

Some examples of sales paradigms that I have found:

- I am not good at sales
- I do not think this is for me
- My people are not interested
- My people are different
- I ran out of leads
- Nobody will believe me
- My product is not the best
- Nobody will pay that price
- People will think that I am crazy
- I can't touch my network
- I am burned out

- People don't take me seriously
- I am not as good as _____
- I am not good with people
- I don't have the power to convince people as _____ does
- My people don't have that kind of money
- I don't have a nice website

What about you? Is success in your sales career at your fin-gertips but your paradigms are holding you back?

You must be open to change your paradigm so you can have permanent results. When that shift happens, everything be-comes different. You gain confidence in yourself. You are able to have valuable conversations and connect with people.

Can you see it? The reason people do not buy from you is not that you are not marketing your product or service well. While marketing will certainly help in the process, marketing alone will not increase your sales.

A couple of months ago I received a request for a consulta-tion from a Dental Office. They had a marketing firm, but they wanted to know more about our services.

As soon as I received the request, I personally sent a text mes-sage to the founder. "Hi, this is Jessica. I'm excited to meet you and mastermind about your potential opportunities to grow your practice".

That text message started a relationship with the founder-the decision-maker. We scheduled our meeting and I came to their office.

I had reviewed their online presence, potential opportunities to rank better in Google, their message, pictures, frequency of content production, and their social media distribution strategy. I had a list of all the mechanics that I had identified that could improve. However, my meeting would not be about my findings. It is quite the opposite. In fact, the meeting was very much like a doctor-patient conversation.

I lead the meeting with questions that were deep into the real story about their dental practice. Their passion for their industry. My questions were something in the lines of:

- How long have you been practicing and what keeps you motivated?
- What does the ideal client look like?
- Which efforts have you done in the past to attract those clients?
- What do you think about the prior efforts? What do you feel is missing?

Are you noticing that I am leading the conversation with open questions? Each answer turned into another question. I made sure that I was taking good notes and writing "keywords" that the dentist was using to describe her services.

I was basically ruling out different strategies while conducting my very own "Visibility Assessment". When I felt that I had gathered enough information about their passion, their message, and the ideal client, I then asked them to go to their computer and see their website.

We went through the list of potential opportunities to improve.

We discussed different scenarios of marketing campaigns. I made sure that I showed them what other leaders in their industry were doing and why those strategies were effective.

At the end of our meeting, the dentist told me "I have had dozens of conversations with marketers, but nobody had taken the time to ask the questions that you asked me today. I felt that you read me very well."

I left that meeting with a verbal commitment. Just one meeting.

When you lead your sales meetings, you are the expert. Just like when you go to the doctor or to the lawyer. You get to tell them your story and they tell you their opinion. You can take it for good or go to a second opinion.

Think about sales as a consultative process. You do not hear your lawyer saying, "we have a 'two-for-one' sale going on". Can you imagine how awkward that would be?

When I worked as an attorney, I would not have liked my clients to say that they hired me because I was the cheapest. I wanted them to hire me because they felt that I was the best option.

You are the leader of that consultation. You are the one who creates a plan and discusses ways to get your potential clients the best results possible. Even if you are selling physical products, you can grow your business with the same mindset. People buy people.

Do you notice a shift in your perception of you as a salesperson? I encourage you to take some notes.

Sales is a skill. You will be surprised ... Perhaps you already have the most important set of skills that the best salespeople have. People skills! As long as you know how to connect with people and make your conversations genuinely about them, not about you, you will be in business.

Niche Marketing

After testing hundreds of social media campaigns, we realized that users engaged more when the content was tailored to their niche.

Marketing to your niche increases the likelihood that you will reach your target audience. It also provides natural guidance for specializing your products and services and narrows your competition. But not only that, niche marketing will provide a higher return on investment since you are already "preaching to the choir."

When your users can feel related to you, they like you. Sooner than later, they will trust you and buy from you. It will be a matter of when not if.

Exercise 1: How to Find Your Niche in 2 Steps

If you are struggling with finding your niche, this exercise can help you tremendously!

Step 1: Three Things About You

Pretend that we are having a face-to-face conversation and I am a potential best partner for you. What 3 things would you want me to know about who you are?

Example using my very own answers:

1) I want you to know that I am a business nerd and I am fascinated about teaching marketing & sales to solopreneurs and freelancers.
2) I want you to know that I am a lawyer-turned-marketer.

3) I want you to know I was born in one of the happiest places in the world and that gave me magnetic genes!

My three things are: "teaching marketing & sales strategy", "lawyer-turned-marketer and educator", and "energetic personality from Puerto Rico".

How about YOU? What do you want me to know about YOU? What are your three things?

You might want to ask for some feedback!

Step 2: Your Niche

Now that you embrace YOU in three words, think about which users will really appreciate connecting with you.

Try to complete this!

From the _____ (big industry), those interested in (interests, hobbies, passions) _____, _____, and _____ will be the most passionate about connecting with someone like me: _____, _____, and _____ (insert your three things here).

Most likely, they call themselves:

_____

_____

_____

Using my example,

From the small business owners industry, those who want to grow a business without sacrificing their family, want to learn marketing secrets, and are into intentional living, will be the most passionate about connecting with someone like me: "teaching marketing & sales strategy", "lawyer-turned-marketer and educator", and "energetic personality from Puerto Rico".

Most likely, they consider themselves:

- ◆ *Content writers*
- ◆ *Bloggers*
- ◆ *Leaders*

You truly want to have conversations with those who are naturally passionate about the topic that you are sharing. They will feel like "you get them".

Now that you have your three words, niche and storyboard, if you already have social media channels, it is time for a cleanup.

What Goes Out	What Stays
Images that are not in alignment with your three powerful words. Remember that visuals create awareness more than words.	Content that has great validation such as comments and shares.
If you have a great visual, but the caption is not speaking to your niche, archive and save it to repost.	From your top 10 posts based on reach, consider leaving them, unless they are not serving your niche.
Repetitive content	Content that builds your credibility.
Boring content	Freebies that are giving you leads.

What Goes Out	What Stays
Inconsistent content	Be open to repurposing what has given you leads and sales.
Confusing content	Anything that makes you say, "heck yes, this is totally me".

Exercise 2: Your Branding Guide

Most people focus solely on the visual aspect of their personal brand. Of course, you want to represent your brand with a beautiful logo, website, and business cards; but that is not the only thing you need.

Why are brand guidelines important?

Think of your brand identity as your company's personality. It is how the world recognizes you and begins to trust you. If you see someone change how they look and act all the time, you will not feel like you know who they are, and you certainly would not trust them.

Before you create a style guide, you need to know your brand. There are five key components:

1. Mission
2. Vision
3. Target audience
4. Brand personality
5. Core values.

Together, these are the most important things needed to establish your brand identity because they tell the world what you stand for.

All the other parts of your brand style guide are tangible elements that communicate those key components to the world through design.

Your Brand Personality

Brand personality is a set of human characteristics that are attributed to a brand name. A brand personality is something to which the consumer can relate; an effective brand increases its brand equity by having a consistent set of traits that a specific consumer segment enjoys. This personality is a qualitative value-add that a brand gains in addition to its functional benefits.

Your brand message has a voice and tone.

It is not about what you say, it's about how you say it. Your personal brand's tone of voice will inform all of its written copy, which includes the website, emails, social media, and overall packaging.

Examples of Brand Personalities

Customers are more likely to purchase a brand if its personality is similar to their own.

5 Main Types of Brand Personalities

1. Excitement: carefree, spirited, and youthful
2. Sincerity: kindness, thoughtfulness, and an orientation toward family values
3. Ruggedness: rough, tough, outdoorsy, and athletic
4. Competence: successful, accomplished and influential, highlighted by leadership
5. Sophistication: elegant, prestigious, and sometimes even pretentious

JESSICA CAMPOS
MARKETING FOR GREATNESS

Dove, for example, chooses sincerity as its brand personality to attract feminine consumers. Luxury brands, such as Michael Kors and Chanel, aim for sophistication. Their brand personality focuses on an upper-class, glamorous, and trendy lifestyle, which attracts a high-spending consumer base. REI, the outdoor recreation retail store, has a rugged brand personality; they focus on inspiring their audience—who are typically outdoorsy, adventurous people—to be strong and resilient.

Don't Overthink It- Plan a Pre-Launch Marketing

Hey... I am interrupting this part of the lesson because I told you I was going to be practical here.

When it comes to branding, I wish I could tell you otherwise, but digital marketing is always a tedious, never-ending project. In other words, you will never feel like you are done.

Take perfectly imperfect action, please!

You can make it easier and even scalable by developing effective pre-launch marketing.

Pre-launch marketing has two main goals:

- Build interest and buzz for the upcoming project.
- Pre-plan your future marketing by knowing who is helping you, who you are going to reach out to, which platforms are going to be more effective, and how exactly you will utilize each of your marketing channels.

Your circle of trust can help you tremendously. You might be very well connected and perhaps, just a few calls will give you a great start. But... we can't just plan for luck. This is where pre-launch marketing comes handy.

Adopt a pre-launch conversation and let those future clients know that they will be getting first-movers' advantages. This works tremendously!

If you see the Branding Map, once you get your first group of clients, you just keep the hustle! Keep polishing your brand. Look at your best clients and define your brand as an experience. Find inspiration from brands that you admire, but always keep your eyes open to ways to raise the bar when it comes to giving your clients positive experiences.

The beautiful thing about having a personal brand is that YOU get to decide! It is your brand, your voice, your message, your personality. The last thing you want is to sound like a second-rate version of another brand.

If you already have quite a bit of content out there, once you have a branding guide, do an Internet audit of everything under your personal brand.

Be sure to conduct a thorough sweep of these channels:

- Your LinkedIn profile
- Your Facebook profile
- Reviews
- YouTube
- Google your name

Assess how your brand is showing up online. Update any incorrect information, polish up your platforms, and remove anything that is no longer aligned with the brand you want to build.

If you are starting from scratch, it will be easier because you would have determined much of the content, tone, and voice and start building on a solid foundation.

PART 3

How To Write So They Engage

If you were to learn "how to write for sales", you will find this popular method called AIDA.

Here's what the AIDA Formula is in a nutshell:

Attention: Get their attention with something catchy and relevant.

Interest: Tell them interesting facts or uses.

Desire: Make them desire the product/service.

Action: Get them to take action.

The problem is that The AIDA model was developed by the American businessman, E. St. Elmo Lewis, in 1898 😵. The original main purpose was to optimize sales calls, specifically the interaction between seller and buyer concerning the product.

While I think the AIDA method is a great start, our digital-everything world brings challenges that didn't exist back in 1898.

You might not know the identity of your future client, but you certainly can use data to know what will move them to like your brand, trust, and take action. This thought process is the backbone of your writing process.

We call it *the future buyers' journey*.

Writing so that People Read and Engage Is Not About Pretty Words

I made this mistake for many years! I thought that I was not a good writer since English is my second language. I thought that writers were people with rich vocabulary, fancy words, and insurmountable adjectives that I cannot even pronounce!

The great news! You do not need to be an amazing writer in order to write copy that sells.

The best writers are the ones who know how to listen to their readers! Oh... wait! So... you might need to read this again. The best writers are the ones who know how to listen to their readers!

If you write, using the words that users understand, easily, you can get them to take action.

Did you know that Google now processes over 40,000 search queries every second on average (visualize them here), which translates to over 3.5 billion searches per day and 1.2 trillion searches per year worldwide?

Why is this relevant? Google has data, so you do not have to create fancy words.

If you know your future users, you can use some of Google's free resources like Google Trends, for example, to know exactly the words they type when they need to find information.

Emotional Marketing

Humans are inherently emotional beings. They like to feel and, when they do, they also like to share it with their friends and family across their social networks. That is the most fundamental reason why social media networks thrive.

But there are some kinds of posts that get more attention on social networks a lot more than others.

The underlying reason is that they instigate the reader to feel a particular emotion strongly. As crazy as it sounds, great marketing requires you to study psychology and human behavior.

Most of us have the same basic mental triggers which drive action. Knowing what those triggers are and how to position them to reach the desired response is extremely important in marketing.

Consumers desire products and services that help them:

1. Save time
2. Save money
3. Save effort
4. Make money

To get them to think about their desires, we need to trigger emotions. Emotion is what really drives the purchasing behaviors and decision-making in general.

Emotional marketing can be immensely powerful — for both brands and consumers.

Emotional marketing refers to marketing and advertising efforts that primarily use emotion to make your audience notice, remember, share and buy. Emotional marketing typically taps into a singular emotion, like happiness, sadness, anger, or fear, to elicit a consumer response. (HubSpot)

Depending on your product, industry, and audience, you cannot always target general "happiness." Like with your marketing goals, you must dig deep and define precisely what feeling you are aiming to elicit. This will influence the details of your marketing — your copywriting, media, graphics choices, etc. — and help it be as effective as possible.

Why Emotional Marketing Works

People feel. As much as we wish we did not, say after a heartbreak or during a scary movie, we cannot help but experience emotions. It is in our nature.

This is one of the reasons emotional marketing just works. Here are a few others.

Emotional marketing makes great first impressions.

In your opinion, what makes for a great first impression? When you meet someone new, what is it that stands out? It is all about how you felt, isn't it?

Now consider a new business. If it were between two advertisements — one that simply talked about products, and one that made you laugh or cry — which would "impress" you? The second one, right?

Emotional marketing can be called right-brain marketing

Right and left-brain differences are what make our brains unique and each of the right and left-brain characteristics play a big role in helping us to make a decision. Most of us find one side of the brain more dominant, leading to understanding which side of the brain may take charge when coming to decisions. With most of the population being left-brain dominant allowing their rational side to take charge, most make realistic and rational decisions. But sometimes using the intuitive right brain may be of assistance.

So, when faced with having to determine which way you need to turn the next time you are lost, you can go with your gut reaction, or take a moment to work out your decision-making process.

When it came down to the wire, how did you decide which option to buy? Better yet, what made you finally click "buy"? (Because let's be real, you probably have bought something online.)

Sure, you compared prices and spent time reading about each product, but when it was time to decide, I'm betting you relied on your heart over your head.

Writing Is Not Just About Pretty Words

Some copywriting experts might claim that writing is a true art. Well, maybe it is art; However, in my opinion, we can argue that it isn't.

Writing is persuasion. Persuasion is science. The science of persuasion or Science of Influence comes from social psychology.

Books and Influence: *Influence: The Psychology of Persuasion* by Robert Cialdini shows us how we can develop our communication skills in order to influence the decisions of individuals. Robert Cialdini is a professor of social psychology at Arizona State University and has conducted a series of investigations on the operation of persuasion in real life.

The Psychology of Sympathy/Like-ability

Cialdini said:

We are more likely to be influenced by the people we like.

If you like someone you are more likely to do something they want or ask. This principle is also based on something as superficial as the physical appearance of a person.

Companies that use sales agents within their community use this principle with great success. People are more likely to buy from people like themselves, friends, and people they know and respect. That is why it is so important to study your potential customers.

Sympathy is the key to selling. Someone will rarely buy something from someone they do not like.

This principle can be applied to Social Media Marketing as follows:

A brand that wants to increase their conversion rates, should simply focus on creating a beautifully executed page with elements that make the visitor *feel represented* by images, colors, words, and the *people* presented in your content.

This is why you will see in our templates, "show and tell" strategies. The idea is that potential buyers can find similarities between you and them. This easily makes customers feel a connection with someone or something they like and that represents them.

The Psychology of Reciprocity

If a request is preceded by an unexpected gift, it has a greater probability to convince potential customers. The gift will make them feel the importance of returning or reciprocating the favor.

Social norms compel us to respond to a favor with another favor, in order to not be considered ungrateful. Think about your daily life... Isn't it easier to get a person to do you a favor after you have given them a gift or done something for them? That feeling of obligation makes them more inclined to agree to your request.

An initial favor will be reciprocated many times over in the future.

For that reason, we encourage you to do more giveaways and freebies!

The Psychology of Authority

People, in general, tend to obey authority figures, even if those authority figures are questionable.

It is just human nature.

When customers feel unsure about a purchase, they usually look for a testimony from a "person with authority on the subject" to serve as a guide. That is why the opinion of professionals or experts is already a classic in the world of advertising.

Pro Tip:

If an authority figure or a leader in your industry has made a positive comment about your product or service, make it known by showing it on your landing page or your pricing page. It will help increase your sales!

The Psychology of Scarcity

With this principle of the Science of Persuasion, people have to know that they are going to miss it if they don't act quickly. It mainly relies on the fact that things are more attractive when their availability is limited, or when we risk losing the opportunity to acquire them.

The law of supply and demand plays a big role in the principle of scarcity. If the customer perceives a low supply or high demand for a good, they will show that they are immediately interested and even willing to pay a higher price. Opportunities seem more valuable when we find it harder to get them.

Cardini developed six principles of persuasion that show you how you can apply them to your business or marketing strategy! You might want to learn more about them!

Cardini's 6 Principles of Persuasion

1. Reciprocity
2. Consistency
3. Social Proof
4. Sympathy/Like-ability
5. Authority
6. Scarcity

While I would love to keep expanding on the topics of persuasion and influencer marketing, I pledged to keep this book as a playbook and be practical. So... let's keep going!

Recap of the Science of Writing

By now you know that social media marketing is about human connections. You know that you have the power to design the brand of YOU and pick the voice and tone that can help you persuade your future buyers.

You also know some pointers from the science of persuasion, so you can generate conversions from social media marketing.

PART 4:

The Playbook to Write Your Copy for Social Media Marketing

First, think about the audience you want to connect with and how they would prefer to engage with you. UX mapping, also known as customer journey mapping, is a powerful technique for understanding what motivates your customers—their needs, hesitations, and concerns.

The best way to connect with your audience on social media is by mapping their experience, all while considering each stage of their decision-making process. To keep this simple, we will narrow the decision-making process into three stages:

Awareness: People have either become aware of your product or service, or aware that they have a need that must be fulfilled.

Evaluation: People are aware that your product or service could fulfill their needs, and they are trying to determine whether you are the best fit. Users turn into leads.

Purchase: This is the stage where they are ready to buy from you. They need information about how to purchase, delivery, etc.

Unlike an in-person visit, users who engage with your brand digitally don't follow a linear order. Some users will find you on Facebook and will check your cover pictures while others will go to your stories. Some users came to your social media channel because a friend sent them. Others came from a search.

The bottom line: your users are in different stages.

Because you can't tell if you will have users on your Instagram on Monday at 7 AM who are seeing you for the very first time, or if most of your users will be considering buying from you at that time, your content needs to consistently market for the three stages: awareness, evaluation, and purchase.

I planned this content so you can have 52 weeks, each week with three posts alternating the three stages.

Short Captions vs Long Captions

You will be surprised here! While short captions can attract followers and give you likes, long-form captions convert more. This is because the "story" you tell is just as important as the images and videos you share – it provides context, adds personality, and can even inspire your followers to take action.

Long captions are great because they allow your audience to learn more about you, your brand and your mission.

Instagram Captions Length

Gone are the days where a pose, a filter, and a short caption would turn users into customers. Users want to connect with you! And, of course, the science of persuasion tells us the kind of content that will make them buy from you!

It seems like the recommended caption length is just under 500 characters, without including the hashtags. Source: Later.com

My Hero Method to Write Long Captions

To simplify this process, I have done this hero method so you can just plug your ideas here and start building your writing muscle!

One thing – I am assuming that you are clear about the brand of YOU, your voice, tone, etc.! If you are not, go back up and read the first two parts of this book!

I am also assuming that you took the time to think about those clients of yours and what they have in common, so you can market to attract people just like them! This is part of your strategy!

Now, let's get to the five elements of the hero method.

The Hero Method To Writing Long Form Captions

1. The emotion

2. The hook

3. The challenge

4. The meat

5. The sense call to action

JESSICA CAMPOS
MARKETING FOR GREATNESS

1. The Emotion

Take some time to think about the emotion you want to trigger in your users.

Is it happiness, sadness, anger, or fear? Do you want to elicit a consumer response, such as "WOW!"?

Producing marketing that creates an emotional response, which creates that 'WOW!' will make customers feel good about doing business with you now and into the future.

Make sure your advertising makes your business memorable for the right reasons and avoid being predictable.

2. The Hook

The one headline that will make users stop scrolling. Sometimes this "hook" can also be part of your visuals. Videos and GIFs are great showstoppers!

3. The Challenge

Be a challenger! Throw a punch to show what you know- from the challenger point of view.

What does it mean to be a Challenger?

Challengers refer to sales reps who follow the powerful Challenger Sales Model from Gartner.

Challengers have different views of the world, understand the customer's business, love to debate, and push the customer.

Introduce this powerful sales technique into your marketing copy. This, in fact, will increase your persuasion by turning yourself into an authority.

Pro tip: do not just do mini-blogs on social media. Use long-form articles, infographics, whitepapers, and books to build your authority profile.

4. The Meat

This is what you want your users to learn from you. Your "meat" is the content you described in the hook.

5. The Sense Call to Action

The Sense Call to Action also comes from the Challenger sales method.

The Gartner Sense Making approach is predicated on the careful sharing of information to guide customers toward a clearer, more rationalized view of the purchase decision.

Instead of asking your readers for a call to action, you will persuade them with what makes sense.

You are now ready for the exciting part!

Now that you understand the basics behind the "why" and the "how" behind using social media in your business, let's save you countless hours.

How to Use this Plug N' Play Content- Ready for You!

Remember when we talked about the importance of mapping your audience experience, all while considering each stage of their decision-making process?

We narrowed the decision-making process into three stages:

- **Awareness**: People have either become aware of your product or service, or aware that they have a need that must be fulfilled.
- **Evaluation**: People are aware that your product or service could fulfill their needs, and they are trying to determine whether you are the best fit. Users turn into leads.
- **Purchase**: This is the stage where they are ready to buy from you. They need information about how to purchase, delivery, etc.

In theory, pretty visuals and amazing content should boost your social media presence and your sales. But this statement is only true if your social media marketing is meeting those expectations *in the eyes of your audience.*

Although it might feel like you need a lot of intuition and creativity to succeed at social media marketing, there is actually a structure you can follow to map your strategy very accurately for your lead nurturing campaigns.

Once you have mapped your user experience, the next step is to apply those insights to strategize your social media content for every stage of the customer journey or buying cycle.

Start with the big picture

It takes a village to achieve the pinnacle of productivity, espe-cially for the intentional CEO who is also, most of the time, a Chief Everything Officer.

This Visibility Playbook goes along with my Visibility Planner, to help you focus on the most important things in your busi-ness- and in your life.

I recommend you take some time to work on the branding exercises I have created for you, to get clarity around your message, so that planning your content becomes easy.

Add your brand voice

Your brand voice already exists; you just have to identify, ar-ticulate, and share it with the world.

I hope that the branding exercises have given you a jump-start so you can discover your unique niche and voice.

Strategic content

I called this Playbook the *Plug N' Play* way to write your content for social media, not because it gives you templates that you can copy and paste, but because it follows a certain rhythm that matches our winning social media marketing strategy.

You now have the opportunity to *plug* these content strat-egies for the entire 52 weeks. You may use them all or just a few of them. The only thing I will emphasize is that your social media content needs to consider the three stages of your audience and that is why we alternate between content to generate likeability, content to ignite conversations, and content to get conversions.

One last thing... remember that conversions on social media are not just about clients. A connection who shows genuine interest in working with you counts as a conversion.

Week 1

Motivational Diary

STRATEGY:

Inspire and humanize your brand.

TEMPLATE:

Day #___ of our Motivational Diary! If you're up to some positivity, keep reading!

Today's topic is how _____. You can be going through____ and still remain positive. You might need ____ and not even know it.

The beauty of life is ____.

So choose to be positive and happy as much as possible.

If we have never met before but you're up to some _____ and tips about _____, let's connect!

PS- You can always edit my settings to follow my ____. We share _____ (describe the content).

Expert Secret

STRATEGY:

You want to showcase how much you know!

TEMPLATE:

Experts say that ___% of people _____ (describe the failures). But that's because (describe the poor choices they make).

I was one of the __% and I can sincerely tell you, I felt ...

*Add bullets describing emotions

Things that have helped me:

*Solution 1

*Solution 2

* Solution 3

I'm very passionate about this topic, as you can tell.

Feel free to ask me anything here!

Reasons Why

STRATEGY:

Since you are establishing a relationship with your audience, today is a good day to educate them on what you do.

TEMPLATE:

Three reasons why you need our _____(describe the service).

Number one:

Number two:

Number three:

I'm a bit biased, but we are just the best in _____, especially because _____.

We are offering ____ until _____ so, if you were waiting for a sign, this is it! Check our link in BIO or DM us!

Week 2

National Holiday

STRATEGY:

Ignite conversations!

TEMPLATE:

It's National ____ (pick a National Holiday from the sociable calendar https://nationaltoday.com/)

Say how are you celebrating it!

Show And Tell

STRATEGY:

Build credibility.

TEMPLATE:

Pick something from your workspace and show it to your fans.

So... it's time for some show and tell. This is ___ and is one of my favorites ____ (share a story).

Who else has a _____?

Appreciation Challenge

STRATEGY:

Share a testimonial indirectly.

TEMPLATE:

#AppreciationChallenge accepted! We want to share our appreciation for _____ (pick a client or a partner). _____(name) we are so proud of your amazing journey. Keep going!

(You can share a before-after image or a written testimonial from your client).

(Close the post with an invitation)

Your transformational story could be next! Currently offering _____ (showcase a promo).

Week 3

What Are Your Plans

STRATEGY:

Create the "I like you effect".

TEMPLATE:

Up and ready to go! We are so looking forward to ___ (describe your plans).

Make sure your content has your unique voice. This dictates your vibe and your vibe attracts your tribe.

What's the Difference Between (Service 1) and (Service 2)

STRATEGY:

Be the Challenger! Educate your users about your services.

TEMPLATE:

97% of small business owners fail, but it's not because of what you think.

We used to think that small business owners failed because of cash flow. We thought that if they had more budget to market, they could succeed.

Wrong.

Success is much more than having a budget to run your business.

It's about knowing how to avoid ____.

Having access to tools that can help a business ___ fast.

It's about timing and people.

Would it make sense to book a call to explore if we are able to customize a plan designed to double your revenue?

Congrats Post

STRATEGY:

Celebrate the progress of your client!

TEMPLATE:

Cheers to ___! Today, (describe accomplishment)! No more ____ (painful times)l! Yay! Well done!

What Do I Do?

STRATEGY:

Use this post to educate your followers about what you do.

Use associations.

TEMPLATE:

"I'm like the doctor for _____". I take care of people who (describe pain) and want (describe their aspiration).

Now over to you! What do you do?

#TBT

STRATEGY:

Build your trust.

Share a picture of when you were in college or getting your certification, program, degree, etc.

Was it hard?

Did you get accolades?

Show!

TEMPLATE:

#TBT from our days at _____. Good times! Hard work pays off!

Letter from a Customer

STRATEGY:

Show your fans how much your current customers love working with you.

TEMPLATE:

"Dear ___, I just want to say thanks for our call. I've been wanting to (describe their aspiration) and finally found you! Loved how _____ (describe aspects that make you unique)."

-Jim

PS- (call to action)

Announce a Series!

STRATEGY:

Generate consistent viewers.

TEMPLATE:

#____Mondays

Today we are launching our #___Mondays! We just want to give you a bunch of (describe what's in there for them).

This series will happen (explain when and at what time).

Industry News

STRATEGY:

Generate authority.

TEMPLATE:

_____ Journal just confirmed that _____. (Share your opinion).

Here's what I know:

*Point 1

*Point 2

*Point 3

(Discuss with your audience and ask for their opinion)

Before and After

STRATEGY:

Generate interest in working with you.

TEMPLATE:

Today we're featuring our _____ (call your clients by a name). She's celebrating her _____ (benchmark).

(How do you feel about this story? Share it!)

Week 6

Series Part 2

STRATEGY:

Generate consistent viewers.

TEMPLATE:

#____Mondays

Remember last week? (Recap)

So... this week (introduce the topic)

Checklist

STRATEGY:

Freebies!

TEMPLATE:

Prepare a visual with an amazing checklist that adds value to your audience.

Remind your audience to save it!

Promo 1 of 3

Announce this campaign! Tell your audience the duration of your promo or your sale.

You have earned permission to ASK your audience. Not only share your promo but ask them "who do you know who needs ____?"

Week 7

Series Part 3

STRATEGY:

Generate consistent viewers.

TEMPLATE:

#____Mondays

Remember last week? (Recap)

So... this week (introduce the topic)

Career Update

STRATEGY:

Build trust. Show your accolades.

TEMPLATE:

It's been an incredible journey. I spent nearly___ years working for (what did you do).

Describe your progress and be thankful.

Promo 2 of 3

Follow up again! Share an update!

You have earned permission to ASK your audience. Not only share your promo but ask them "who do you know who needs ____?"

Week 8

Series Part 4

#____Mondays

Remember last week? (Recap)

So... this week (introduce the topic)

What's coming up next?

Pre-Promo

STRATEGY:

Pre launch!

Since you have a promotion ON, use this opportunity to share a preview of what your audience can get from your promo!

Tease them!

TEMPLATE:

We can barely wait to show you what we've been working on!

Promo

STRATEGY:

Offer an irresistible bonus.

TEMPLATE:

*** EXCITING NEW PROJECT ANNOUNCEMENT ***

Over the years, a lot of you have been asking how I create and develop my designs, and many have requested specific design courses. Today, I can announce that I have something better in store for you.

.

For the past __ years, I have been developing and crafting my very own design process to streamline and optimize my creative workflow.

.

For the past __ years, I have been tweaking, modifying, adding and refining it. This process has liberated me from the stress and anxiety of time management and any struggles I used to have with generating creative ideas and presenting to clients.

.

My current design process allows me to:

.

Minimum stress,anxiety & wasted time

.

Maximum creativity & results

.

In recent years it has really started to pay off. Today, my design process guarantees that I process enough information, undertake enough discovery, generate many interesting ideas, and develop good design to deliver a fantastic creative solution.

.

In gratitude to all of you, I would like to give you a free digital version of this design! All you need is to leave me a comment here or if it makes sense, go to the link in BIO.

-

Week 9

View From the Office Today

STRATEGY:

Generate the "I like it" factor.

TEMPLATE:

This is what my work station looks like these days

What You Don't Know That You Don't Know

STRATEGY:

Generate the *I trust in you* factor.

TEMPLATE:

Showcase your expertise and give your audience specific details that you know! Prompt them with "did you know that ____?"

Partner Shout Out

STRATEGY:

Market the experience.

Today you're featuring a vendor, partner, or someone who collaborates with your business. Make it about them!

TEMPLATE:

Would you please help us say congrats to our friends over _____ business. We've been in business together since ____. They are our _____.

Teamwork makes the dream work!

Week 10

Enneagram (Something Personal About You)

STRATEGY:

Build more opportunities to find things that you have in common with your audience.

TEMPLATE:

Let's talk ENNEAGRAM!!! ▢▢▢**What's your enneagram # and do you feel like it portrays you accurately??**▢

▢▢▢▢

I am a type 7 which is the enthusiast!

Some words to describe 7's are:_____. (WOW so true)!▢
▢▢▢

▢▢▢▢

A 7's basic desire is "_____." ▢▢▢▢ *A 7's basic fear is "_____."*▢▢▢▢

▢▢▢▢ *(Share your personality trait)*

Self Discovery

STRATEGY:

Freebies help you build authority.

Template

Are you wondering if you're ready to switch careers? If so, this quiz can help you get closer to making such a difficult decision.

Take it and feel free to connect with me if you want to discuss your results!

Demo
....

STRATEGY:

Can you share a demo of your services? A video will be great!

TEMPLATE:

Use TikTok and do a tour showing them a product, or your location!

Book Review

. . . .

STRATEGY:

Share one of your favorite book reviews! To ignite conversations.

TEMPLATE:

I've found a love for reading again whilst in isolation, and as I tend to read things that are linked to psych in some way, I thought I'd share my thoughts about them here.

I will not be giving away any spoilers, just a brief overview and why I'd recommend (or not!!)

-- Share your opinion!

The Contrarian ...

. . . .

Is there a popular practice in your industry that you simply don't believe? Share here why!.

I was completely _____ and_____ (what happened), I just couldn't _____.

Best Decision Ever

. . . .

STRATEGY:

Building credibility.

Can we share a story from a client of yours who is happy that they hired you?

TEMPLATE:

Best decision ever! Before working with ____ I was _____ (describe the challenges). After ____ later, I am _____ (describe the wins).

Week 12

Weekend Recap

STRATEGY:

Take your audience to your personal life a bit!

TEMPLATE:

Sharing some of our great moments from the weekend. We had such a great time! .... (Explain with details!)

This Time Last Year...

This time last year we were (describing a great thing that happened).

Take your audience along your journey!

Giveaway Time (Pre-Launch)

Tease your audience about your giveaway plans!

♡ G I V E A W A Y ♡

What better way to kick off_____ than with a giveaway.

What you'll win

How to win

Official giveaway will be on ____. (Next week)

Week 13

Quote

Think about the audience you want to hold captivated for your giveaway and inspire them with a quote.

Templates:

A girl should be two things: classy and fabulous.

Coco Chanel.

In order to be irreplaceable one must always be different. Coco Chanel.

Why Is It This Instead of That?

Think about a common mistake your target audience makes. Why do they make that mistake? What can they do to avoid it?

Every ____ thinks that their best way to succeed at ____ is by ____.

Guess what? (Describe how you discovered the huge mistake).

So... no, the best way to ____ is by:

Number 1

Number 2

Number 3

Number 4

(Create a mini slideshow for visuals)

Giveaway Time

♡ G I V E A W A Y ♡

What better way to kick off_____ than with a giveaway.

We partnered with @_____ to give one lucky winner a_____ ✨

To enter:

♡ Like this photo ♡ Follow @_____ & @_____

♡ Tag as many friends as you want on this post (1 comment = 1 entry)

♡ BONUS: get 10 extra entries when you share this post to your stories, tag us both, & mention the giveaway! (Public accounts only)

〰️

Giveaway is open WORLDWIDE 🌎 and will run until_____.

Winner will be announced on stories the following Friday. This giveaway is not affiliated with Instagram. Good luck!! 🏵️

Week 14

Vulnerable Post

STRATEGY:

Building a personal connection with your audience.

TEMPLATE:

"Give yourself permission to stop trying to be perfect"

This quote HIT ME yesterday! Sometimes I catch myself being so hard on myself when there are toys everywhere, laundry needs to be folded, dishwasher needs to be emptied (why does this take me forever BTW?)... then I remember..

How To

How to _____ (explain) in ___ steps.

Pro tip: add infographics to this explainer post!

Giveaway Winner

♡ G I V E A W A Y ♡ winner announcement!!!!

Week 15

Netflix

STRATEGY:

Building a personal connection with your audience.

TEMPLATE:

So, I've been watching _____. Anyone else? I'm not up to spoil it, but WOW, so far, I'm giving this one _____. Love that _____.

Let me know if you watch it!

The Survey

STRATEGY:

Ignite business conversations.

TEMPLATE:

DYING to know: What industry are you in? A quick response would mean the world to me!

I'd love to create posts specific to your niche, so help me help you.

Indirect Pitch

STRATEGY:

Ignite leads.

TEMPLATE:

Want more (describe what your audience needs) without (their objection)? What if you had the chance to (try your service) and this time it worked?!

You finally get to (how would this change their lives?) _____.

Over the past ___ (years or months) we have helped ____ with their ____.

Maybe this isn't for you, but you know someone who would love to (offer a free consultation). Tag them here!

Week 16

Pet Day

STRATEGY:

Ignite likes and comments.

TEMPLATE:

Hi friends, today I want to introduce _____ to you! _____ has been with me since _____. (Things your pet loves).

A Sales Objection

STRATEGY:

Making your followers think about your services.

TEMPLATE:

How do you know if you're ready for (your services)?

The best way to know is if you (describe emotions of urgency).

If you want to discuss in detail, let's have virtual coffee!

Special Invite!

STRATEGY:

Making your followers consider your services.

TEMPLATE:

Let's (describe the result)!

Wanna know the best way to _____ (describe their pain)? Want an easier way to _____?

The secret to ___ is to ____ and that's exactly what we are doing in our _____.

--Add info to sign up and due date!

Week 17

Goals!

STRATEGY:

Be approachable and market your values.

TEMPLATE:

This morning...

.

Promise yourself that you're going to take big action towards your goals and dreams today!!.

Show and Tell

STRATEGY:

Offer value, not a sale.

TEMPLATE:

Want more _____? Why not _____? Here are a few tips on how I make it happen.

Number 1

Number 2

Number 3

I hope this _____ was helpful. If you liked it, let me know in the comments, so I know to do a future series again soon!

Love Our Reviews

STRATEGY:

Ignite consideration.

TEMPLATE:

Thank you ___ for this amazing review!

Post a loyal client review here.

Announcing a Three-Part Series

STRATEGY:

Build consistent followers.

TEMPLATE:

This 3-part ___ series will lay the framework for _____.

Here's part 1!

Three-Part Series, Part 2

In part 1 of (the series) (posted yesterday), I explained how _____.

In part 2, we dig into ___ questions: ___, _____, and ____.

Three-Part Series, Part 3

Recap of days 1 and 2, and introduce day 3.

Like always, I'd love to hear your feedback or questions, so let's chat below!

Dramatic Joy

STRATEGY:

Promote your business!

TEMPLATE:

Don't wanna be dramatic but I'm jumping of joy with this amazing news: MY NEW _____ LAUNCHES ON _____!

Best Deal Ever

STRATEGY:

Promote your business!

TEMPLATE:

Let's make a deal: Can we trade something?

(Explain how did you come up with the thing you're about to launch)

_____ months later, I've decided to stop making excuses and start having fun.

I know I can totally fail at this. But I'm willing to try.

Can we make a deal? I am willing to trade my fear for fun and launch this _____ thing.

The future is ours for the taking.

Reach out, hold on, and grab tight as it takes you where you want to go.

Are you ready to make this trade?

Office Tour

Take a product or a service on a tour and make an amazing picture.

Today we are taking our ____ to (public and popular location). We totally loved the fact that we get to impact people in _____.

Week 20

National Holiday

STRATEGY:

Pick a relevant holiday to raise awareness for a cause.

TEMPLATE:

Didn't realize it, but I

guess I was waiting for #nationalsiblingsday to announce that:

Charlie has a new baby brother and she's THRILLED!

*Remember to include the relevant #'s. Do your research to see the content that has been previously shared.

Tease Thursday

STRATEGY:

Ignite conversations.

TEMPLATE:

I've got the feeling...!!! (Get your fans in a good mood) and talk about a project you're working on!

You're a click away from your best (describe the experience) ...

We are working hard in the creation of _____.

Those of you who are (industry) and want (solution) without having to _____, doors are opening soon!

Sign up today and get a coupon via email!

You Should Be Here

STRATEGY:

Inspire people.

TEMPLATE:

Show people who they want to be, and associate that person with your product.

Week 21

Big News Monday!

STRATEGY:

You teased your fans, so now it's time for another reveal.

TEMPLATE:

We are SO excited to announce our new LIFESTYLE LINE "___" 😍!!!

.

In addition to our activewear, we will now be releasing everyday wear from jeans, dresses, tops and more 🙌

.

This has been in the making for over a year and has been the absolute hardest to keep secret, but we know you are going to love what we have in store 🔥

.

Featuring our new "_____" paired with our new "_____"

.

Stay tuned for more releases to come 👏

Unboxing Video

STRATEGY:

Here's where you will give them some behind the scenes info to your upcoming launch.

Can you share with them how you came up with the price? What is your number one factor when you pick your services and your offers?

You can say "we believe in quality over quantity (and explain why)."

Today Is The Day!

STRATEGY:

Be consistent with your promise!

TEMPLATE:

Our new ___ is here! Doors are open for those of you who want___.

This opportunity is a great for _____ (describe one of your avatars).

Week 22

Can You Believe It?

STRATEGY:

This is another touch to build relationships. The more things in common you have with your followers the easier it will be to build a relationship.

TEMPLATE:

Share a story about something that used to be an obstacle for you. *Use the Super Hero method to write your long story.*

Pinterest Style

STRATEGY:

Build authority through adding value.

TEMPLATE:

Can you do a quick tutorial on how to ___? Check on Pinterest and get ideas of the infographic!

Use Canva.com to build your own!

Partner Shout Out

STRATEGY:

This is an opportunity to market your experience. Those who are considering doing business with you will feel inspired.

TEMPLATE:

Please celebrate with us! It's _____'s anniversary. We've been doing business since ___.

It's always a pleasure doing business with you!

What Are You Reading?

STRATEGY:

In thought leadership, learning is an ongoing task! It's good to share books you are reading and other resources that are helping you.

TEMPLATE:

Getting ready for a busy week. Speaking of which, have you read ____? I'm getting a lot of great nuggets! Maybe we should do a book club! Curious to know about you!

Homework!

STRATEGY:

Ignite conversations with your audience. Give them homework!

TEMPLATE:

Answer these questions:

What's at stake for me to play BIG?

What's at stake for the world when you play BIG?

Advanced: Do it on Video.

Indirect Pitch

STRATEGY:

Educate your audience about what you do.

TEMPLATE:

When you stress over little details, you miss the big oppor-tunities. What's something about _____ that you stress over?

Just know that we are here to _____ (describe the service).

Our clients get (describe results) in _____ (describe time or effort).

Check the link in BIO to schedule an appointment!

Week 24

Motivational Monday

STRATEGY:

Market your personality!

TEMPLATE:

Monday is a day of new beginnings and fresh starts. It's a day where the week is before you and possibilities are endless. ... So let's make this Monday one of the good ones. One where you demonstrate the power of a positive attitude and rocket toward your goals.

Consider this as an inspiration for your fans!

Trending Post

STRATEGY:

Check in Google Trends what's a hot topic for your industry! Share your opinion about it.

TEMPLATE:

Did you hear the news? I still can't believe that _____.

For us, professional ____, it's hard to ___.

(Express yourself! The idea is to ignite conversations)

Freebie

STRATEGY:

Activate the power of reciprocity. The more you give, the more people want to listen to you.

TEMPLATE:

Buckle up! We want to give our Insta Fam the chance to try our _____ for free!

All you need to do is to comment 🙏 here and we will message you with our _____!!!

Week 25

I Am Ready for More

STRATEGY:

The idea here is to let your audience know that you're growing, but your business is ready for more)

TEMPLATE:

Spending some extra time in reflection and R E S T this week.

As I start to reevaluate how I spend my time and where my energy is being placed, I am slowly learning to differentiate between quality vs quantity living.

As a business owner, our lives are _____. My business has grown ___% in the last ___ days and I'm so honored.

(Tell them some details about the things you are doing to get ready for more).

Birthday Bash

STRATEGY:

Ignite joy! We want to celebrate your business growth. Can you get some balloons, a cupcake or something to show how you are celebrating progress?

TEMPLATE:

We are T H R E E years old today! It's hard to believe we were just _____ (share how you started).

Since then, we've helped over_____ (how many people) people with their (what have they achieved).

We are so thankful to everyone who has supported us! Happy birthday, ____! (business name) 🎉

Birthday Bash DEAL

STRATEGY:

No need to call it "deal" but the idea is to keep consistency with your message, honor your progress, and use it as a reason to announce this deal)

TEMPLATE:

The (business name) turned 2 today! 🎉

Two whole wonderful years of our shop being open!

In honor of our shop's anniversary, we are having a sale!!!!

Get 20% off your entire order AND free shipping on orders $35 or more.

Our sale is going on from 3/6-3/8.

THANK YOU again for all your support, we are so incredibly thankful for all of it! ❤️

Week 26

Feeling Grateful

STRATEGY:

Keep up with your growth story. Your fans love when you make them feel part of your journey.

TEMPLATE:

We/I are so grateful for all the amazing support we have received.

It seriously means so much to us/me.

We/I are looking forward to another amazing year!

We/I have so many new and fun _____ coming your way.

Case Study

STRATEGY:

Case studies help build trust and credibility in what you offer.

Template: (real estate)

The _____ House is on the market in _____.

This house was custom built for the owners. As you can imagine, it had a lot of sentimental value to them.

Here's what we did to get this house on the market:

(Explain the steps).

What do you think of this before and after?

Direct Response Marketing

STRATEGY:

Direct response is the infomercial style. Your goal is to create an instant decision. Great for sales.

TEMPLATE:

Are you into fancy____? 🔥

We're now offering ____ with __% off. If you've been meaning to get your ____ fixed, this is IT!

Remember to use code ____.

(The visual will do 99% of the job!)

Work/Life Balance
....

Strategy

The idea is to establish a deeper connection with your fans.

TEMPLATE:

Let's talk work/life balance 🔘

.

We all have brought work home at some point and I am definitely guilty of doing that.

Being in the ___ field doesn't make it any easier, especially with _____ (describe a challenge).

But here's what I've been doing to reach my work-life balance these days:

.

(Name examples and ask your fans for other ideas).

This Is How We Do It
....

STRATEGY:

Showing the "how" and giving access to "a day in your life" builds trust.

This can be a simple boomerang video of you doing something. Even typing! Show excitement!

TEMPLATE:

Beating the heat with Cooper. #thisishowwedoit

"Need Your Help"

STRATEGY:

Make your fans part of a new project. They feel like you care about them.

TEMPLATE:

We've been sending these ___ to our new clients! They love it and we are so in love too!

Do you have any other ideas for us on how to make our new clients feel appreciated? We are more than happy to establish some collaboration! Please send us suggestions!

Week 28

It's The Season

STRATEGY:

As the season changes, your inspiration changes. Is it time to organize your spaces? Take your audience to your projects!

TEMPLATE:

Who else loves this space? 🌿 🐦 🤍 🪴

I'm so ready for a change (you can mention why and refer to a season). Thinking about something like this for my office. Thoughts?

Guest Speaker

STRATEGY:

Let's showcase your appearance as a guest speaker.

TEMPLATE:

They call me a travel expert on TV, isn't that fun? ⬜ *Chatting holiday travel tips on @_____ there's a little snippet in my portfolio (link in bio) if you want to take a look! happy travels, amigos!* 🎄 📱

Mini Sales Page

Strategy

This is the typical, long call to action.

TEMPLATE:

Do you feel:

☆ *Stuck in the wrong job?*

☆ *Lacking confidence?*

☆ *Unsure how to make your business fly?*

☆ *Like you're holding yourself back?*

☆ *Ready for a new challenge?*

.If you're nodding along, then get yourself booked in on the next round of Step Up School. 🦉 Early Bird offer (that's a whopping 30% off) starts now and ends on Wednesday. 🦉

.

Here's the thing, if you don't invest in yourself and your future, things are never going to change.

Don't wait any longer, come and learn how to overcome your challenges and fulfill your potential again in just 3 days.

Plus, become part of an awesome new female network. This is very much a #WomenSupportingWomen 👭 👭

.

____ Add details of your event.

. ☎️ If you're feeling unsure, book in your free call with me, Alice, by clicking the link in bio ☎️

.

❄️ As one our most recent grads put it: "Step Up School has been the start of a complete change in my life." Now let Step Up School do the same for you! News about our very exciting guest coach to follow ❄️

.

CLICK LINK IN BIO OR DM 👆 *TO BOOK AND FIND OUT MORE.* 👆
🏵

.

Week 29

Mindset Post

STRATEGY:

Opportunity to showcase your values as an individual. Remember, you are speaking to your ONE PERSONA.

TEMPLATE:

✦PROFESSIONAL DEVELOPMENT✦

Since changing to an individual contributor role, I have really missed mentoring and developing other professionals. I've had the chance to do some 1-on-1's over the phone and it has been so wonderful!

✦Since *we're about to have a LOT more time on our hands, I was thinking about setting up a couple phone chats a week with anyone who might still be looking for career advice, interview prep, professional development, or to ask questions!*

✦Is this something you think might be beneficial?

✦If you'd like to set up a 30 minute chat, DM me and I'll see about getting something scheduled! I'll try to do as many as possible!

Here's a Template

STRATEGY:

Sharing freebies is a great way to keep adding value to your fans.

TEMPLATE:

I still can't get enough of these_____. Free template available on my website (link in bio) and when you download, you will get an extra ____ via email!

Reminder

STRATEGY:

When you invite your fans to take an offer, they need to know what's the due date and a reminder, so this is the reminder post.

TEMPLATE:

Don't forget that doors are closing at midnight!

🦉*Early Bird offer (that's a whopping 30% off).* Check the link in BIO and get this today!

Week 30

Mini Blog Post

STRATEGY:

Making your fans aware of your transformation is important so they feel like you "get them". This post is a mini blog.

TEMPLATE:

DECISIONS!

All of your choices have led you to become the person you are today. We are a product of our thoughts and actions.

If you keep doing what you are doing, where will you be in 1, 5 and 10 years from now?

Are your decisions leading you toward the life you want to live and to the person you want to become?

You can literally be, do, and have everything you want in life. It's up to you to decide 🙏

MAKE A DECISION TO CREATE THE LIFE THAT YOU WANT 🏃

New Milestone

Strategy

As a leader in your industry, it's important to showcase your growth. Likes attract likes.

TEMPLATE:

BREAKING NEWS: Allow me to introduce _____ Fitness to you.

I've officially launched my new _____! 🙌

What does this mean for you?

(Tell them how is this different and how can they get this)

To continue with your routine workouts with me, you can do so exclusively by booking and purchasing classes using the MINDBODY app, look for _____. (Or refer them to your link)

Thank you from the bottom of my heart for your support. I am so grateful to be a part of such an incredible fitness community. The excitement that I feel is beyond, and I look forward to starting this new chapter with you!

Share a Private Text

STRATEGY:

Follow up with your message about the new service)

TEMPLATE:

*Have you tried a Virtual Fitness class yet? If you answered no, ask yourself why? What's stopping you? * ***

The message posted above comes from a client who regularly took my in-person classes.

*This weekend I am offering a FREE Full Bodyweight Conditioning class that starts at 10am EST. If you want to join, send me a DM with your email and I'll send you the Zoom link to join the fun! I challenge you to try it and do something out of your comfort zone. Change doesn't come from comfort! **

Week 31

Inspirational Post

STRATEGY:

Inspire people! Find a great visual for this.

TEMPLATE:

Starting is the hardest part. You have to take leap of faith and go for your dreams ♥

Please Help Me Welcoming

STRATEGY:

Show your fans your growth and celebrate exciting news.

TEMPLATE:

📢 GREAT NEWS ALERT 📢

We are happy to announce our newest agent! ▢

A little bit about ___ 😃

Cats or Dogs? ___

Fav Netflix show? ___

Born in ____

Fav trip ___

We are excited that she has joined our team!

This Is Us!

STRATEGY:

Showcase a group -can be your team or group of clients.

TEMPLATE:

There is NO "I" in TEAM 👊👊👊

TEAM – DEFINITION

A group of people with different skills and different tasks, who work together on a common project, service, or goal, with a meshing of functions and mutual support.

Synergy exists, so the team performs in a way that is greater than the sum of its parts.

So much more than a business! Sisterhood is more like it!

Here to serve. If you ever want to chat, DM us!

Week 32

Personal Goals

STRATEGY:

Any fitness goal or another personal goal that you would like to share with your audience? They love getting involved in your progress.

TEMPLATE:

Showed up this morning and did a 30 minute workout before a productive day.

You don't realize how much you've neglected yourself until you make yourself a priority (again).

Working hard and working out go hand-in-hand!

Expert Takeover

STRATEGY:

This post is to bring a new voice to your audience. Ideally you could do a video- interviewing an expert.

TEMPLATE:

I was so nervous, but we did it! (Describe who is in the interview).

Get ready to learn the 10 questions to ask yourself to see better results in your health journey, personal relationships and business.

Podcast/Blog

Persuade people about a challenge and a solution you propose. Take the time to write a great article, podcast or video. Then, introduce your topic and give your fans reasons to read it.

Template: (written in 3rd person)

Building your podcast website with _____.

You've created an awesomesauce podcast but now you realize that getting it out there doesn't just mean adding it to Apple Podcasts or Spotify. 😳 You also need to decide where on the web your podcast will live!

That's what @_____ is here to help with.

She supports entrepreneurs + bloggers like you. Build your website and market yourself online without being techie (or sales-y). 💻 Check out the highlights from our chat on how to build your podcast website!

Want to tune in for the whole conversation? Catch it by subscribing to the secret Bosspod(cast) at (_____).

Tune into the whole interview to discover:

🎞 *If you should have a separate website for your podcast*

🎞 *Where on your website is best to place your podcast*

🎞 *If you should embed the audio of your episodes*

🎞 *How much info on each episode should be on your website*

🎞 *The best way is to send listeners back to your website*

Back to the Future

....

STRATEGY:

Big things are coming your way. Do you have an event coming up? Are you preparing? Do you belong to a community? Share the journey.

TEMPLATE:

Loving what I do and getting ready for more.

.

_____is my biggest blessing, seeing others thrive and become the "better version" is one of my passions in life.

.

It all started a long time ago, I'd say back in 1996 after I became a mother. I used to go to the gym and get bombarded with questions at the ladies room.

.

Today my job is way more sophisticated and highly eclectic, combining much more than the fitness philosophy, or the standard nutritional guidance.

.

Becoming who I am was hard work, years and years of studying and implementation for myself. That's why after the struggle it feels so good to be the one that I've envisioned back on my early beginning.

.

Thank you to all of my students, clients, mentors, and amazing people who had been with me on this journey.

.

More to come!

Meet My Tribe Post
• •

STRATEGY:

Market the experience. Your circle of influence.

TEMPLATE:

Are you craving connection with like-minded women during this time?

Or wanting extra support and love as you navigate all the uncertainty in your life?

We've got you covered!

In one week, I'm hosting a virtual women's circle- so no matter where in the world you are, you can be connected.

There's only 14 spots left, so grab your ticket before they goooo. Link in bio ♡

What Do We Do?
• •

STRATEGY:

Educate your audience about what you do.

TEMPLATE:

"Living the dream." Is what I say every time someone asks me what I do. Can I tell you a little secret? Most people think that I'm a _____. They see me _____ and wearing _____. So I don't blame them.

What do I really do?

I'm a _____. My background is in _____. And I became obsessed with _____ so that's what I do! Mixing my passion for _____ and helping others.

Follow Up - Invite

STRATEGY:

You told them about your Tribe. Share a reminder.

TEMPLATE:

Remember! Our virtual women's circle is happening in 2 days!

There's only 6 spots left, so grab your ticket before they goooo. Link in bio ♡

I Can't Believe- T-1 - The Countdown

STRATEGY:

Let's get your fans to meet you out of social media! Rally your event.

TEMPLATE:

Almost sold out! Are you in? Our virtual women's circle is happening tomorrow and you can still join us.

If you've been wanting extra support and love as you navigate all the uncertainty in your life, this is IT!

Check out the link in bio ♡ *and if you have any questions, DM me!*

Event Recap

STRATEGY:

Show results, let's show you in action.

TEMPLATE:

All the makings of a great event at ___: A Women's Leadership Conference 3.5!

Good content, nourishing food, great local businesses and amazing women. Catch it all in the #___ (recap): Leaders ___ to be Authentic (link in bio).

Week 35

Happy National _____

STRATEGY:

So.... you have been extremely busy and it's time to take a little break! Cool off with a light National Holiday. Show your magnetic personality.

TEMPLATE:

Happy National Doctors Day!!! 🏥😃 *Thankful for all my Physicians friends!*

Happy to be able to serve!

Validating Your Authority!

STRATEGY:

Have you been featured? Time to share it!

TEMPLATE:

My article on staying productive, sane and positive during times of uncertainty.

I shared my three must-have tools for staying focused while working remote with @_____.

Facebook Live Invite

STRATEGY:

Keep inviting your audience to come closer to you!

TEMPLATE:

If you've been wondering about starting a membership site, or whether a membership site could even work for your business, I've got something for you!

Join me TODAY at 4pm PT / 7pm ET on Facebook LIVE talking all about whether adding a membership component to your online business is right for you.

Have any questions? Comment them below and I'll do my best to cover answers during today's live.

Week 36

Here's My Take on Leadership Post

STRATEGY:

Share your ideas about relevant topics. Remember to get conversational.

TEMPLATE:

Hands up if you feel like you're a natural born leader 🙋‍♂️

Hey, where are all the hands? Oh right, maybe 5% of the population feels like they were born to lead. The rest of us happily ignore building up our leadership bones until we can no longer hide from it.

Of course, I'm speaking for myself. My biggest regret in the 10 years of running an online business is not focusing on becoming a better leader.

It's been said many times that entrepreneurship is like getting a PhD in personal development and learning to lead is a huge part of that.

Next level success requires next level leaders. That's why I'm finally learning all I can about how to rise to the occasion.

I just wrote a blog about _____.

Full disclosure: this is one of those episodes where I really open up about where I've missed the mark.

Click the link in BIO to read it!

Money Convo Part 1

STRATEGY:

People who are in consideration need to hear the money conversation!

TEMPLATE:

I hear it all the time when people say, "I don't have the money, I can't afford it." And in saying this, they stop themselves from doing the thing that they really, really want to do, that will move their business and their life forward.

You see, this way of thinking stops women from seeing the opportunities that are all around them. I see people use phrases like, "I need to put a roof over my head," and "I need to be able to put food on the table for my family."

And listen, I get it. There are people who are in REAL poverty in this and many other countries. But I'm not talking about those people.

I'm talking about people who are self-employed who have opportunities to make money all around them, and yet they play the "I'm a victim" card.

So here's what I want to explain (I hope you'll suspend judgment for just a little bit longer). I invite you to start thinking about being RESOURCEFUL.

When the money is not in the bank account, it's absolutely easy to say, "I don't have the money" right away. But you are actually full of money...at least, in terms of opportunities.

So I want you to look around, because there's money in your life right now.

Be resourceful.

If you want something that's a bit out of reach, get scrappy, ask for help. It's all about finding the opportunities around you to bring in the money, and then actioning them.

This is about getting out of your comfort zone. This is about getting scrappy. It's about THE HUSTLE. And every once in a while, that's what's required.

Become resourceful, become creative. Do whatever it takes and you will find the money, and you can afford whatever it is that you want.

Need ideas to FIND MONEY? Let's chat!

Money Convo Retouch

STRATEGY:

A great follow up from the money conversation.

TEMPLATE:

Hey my friend! Just a quick message today to remind you to check your energy. Check yourself before you wreck yourself, right?

Check your energy around the things you say you want in your life or in your business.

I see a lot of people saying, "I need to do this," or "I have to do this." This is your loving reminder to change that from "I have to" or "I need to" into "I get to" instead.

You see, "I get to" is an energy of gratitude instead of struggle. You get to work, you get to do great things.

See the difference?

Have We Met Yet?

Strategy

A very popular post that you can leverage to get to meet your audience.

TEMPLATE:

I'm soooo due to share an introductory post with my new friends.

My name is _____, I'm 37 and I live in Nottingham UK with my partner and our identical twin boys.

My business is _____. I started it back in _____ trying to figure out (describe).

My favorite part of what I do?

___ (describe).

A great introduction or referral for me? _____.

Money Convo Objection Talk

STRATEGY:

Is money the biggest objection? Then, educate your fans about this topic. Be consistent about this topic.

TEMPLATE:

I want to talk to you about MONEY.

You see, money is more than money. It's a story.

And your understanding of your money story has a dramatic impact on your ability to make it and keep it.

All of us received powerful lessons about money when our minds were wide open as children. Before the age of 8, we are literally learning how the world works.

So...

If we are told that making money is bad and that people with money are bad...we believe it and don't want to become that (on a subconscious level).

If we are told that wanting more things (toys, food, etc.) makes us selfish and greedy...we believe it and don't want to become that (on a subconscious level).

If our family didn't have money, we understand that money is for "other people" and don't feel we deserve it (on a subconscious level).

These stories have incredible power over us, because when they remain in our unconscious minds (our mindset), they drive our actions and behaviors. (That's why everything we do at Boldheart leads with shifting our mindset first, then taking action.)

Some people who are making "good money" still struggle with making money.

Some people who are growing their business stay stuck at a certain level because they can't overcome their money story.

If this is you, sweet friend, take some time today to write down your money story.

What are some of the beliefs that you have about money? What was your family's relationship to money? How has money impacted your life to date?

You can do it. I believe in you.

Let's Collab Post

STRATEGY:

Tapping into a marketing partner's audience helps increase your reach and visibility.

TEMPLATE:

This can be a simple selfie showing you in action with a marketing partner.

--Girls setting the world on fire!

(Tag everybody)

Week 38

Expand Professional Associations

STRATEGY:

Keep finding opportunities to connect with your users based on interests.

TEMPLATE:

The moment you find yourself and feel like YOU again!

What I love about this community:

-

-

-

-

This is us! Empowering women is what we do best!

This isn't your traditional networking group! If it makes sense to you, explore _____ (website) and let's have a chat!

The Biggest Obstacle We Had in Our Business and How We Overcame It

STRATEGY:

Build the "you get me" emotion.

TEMPLATE:

Here's a Brand Visibility Checklist I use for my clients who hire me to grow their business !! I'm curious to know what's your next big step based on my checklist !!

✳️ Sometimes you just have to make a bold move and do things YOUR way.

✳️ That's the case for many leaders. Maybe you can't find answers because YOU are called to BE the voice. You are called to BE the BRAND of YOU.

✳️ This roadmap to build the brand of YOU works! The only thing ... your mind might try to sabotage you and you might think:

⚡ Everyone else is doing this.

⚡ I'm late ...

⚡ It's too much work and I don't know ...

⚡ I don't have those credentials

✳️ You get inspired and excited, but you can't turn your ideas into action because there's a tiny bit of doubt that stops you.

✳️ Listen up! We all needed to start somewhere. Knowledge is power. So ... maybe it's true that you don't know it all, but who said you had to?

✳️ Back in 2009 I did the craziest transition ever! Decided to close my law practice to pursue my online business. Was it scary? Yes.

Worth it? Yes! I realized I didn't want to live a life chasing a career path. I wanted a lifestyle. I found a way to merge my calling to help people with my dream to have a family (I had just remarried after being a single mom for 5 years. We then had 3 babies back to back).

Don't be afraid to start! You might want to have access to a business strategy session with me. Let me know when you're ready!

📎 We are running amazing courses! Check link in BIO!

How Soon Will You See Results When You Work With Me?

....

STRATEGY:

This is a follow up from the previous post.

TEMPLATE:

Why do you think you're not making 6-7 figures in business? This story will inspire you!

- Share the story of a client.

- Make them the super hero!

Video IGTV/YouTube

STRATEGY:

Videos help you establish a better connection with your audience.

TEMPLATE:

I'm answering some of your most pressing business questions in this Q&A video.

Questions like:

👉 *How do you find the fortitude to carry on during tough times?*

👉 *How do you stay positive?*

👉 *How do you implement the right processes? Find the right people?*

Grab the link in bio to watch the whole video and subscribe on YouTube.

Have a question I haven't answered yet? Ask away!

*Pro tip: Mention upcoming videos, upcoming tutorials, or events.

Another Case Study!

STRATEGY:

Be strategic. If you have leads "on the fence", prepare a case study thinking about them.

TEMPLATE:

Please help me say congratulations to _____ for achieving top producer this month.

When we started working together, ___ (describe her "before").

2 months later, she's been able to (describe her "after".

I asked her: what would you say to anyone who's struggling with _____ and have been invited to our program?

Her answer: _____.

(Help your audience jump over that fence!).

Three Pivotal Moments that Led Me to Creating [OFFER]

STRATEGY:

Think about your niche and your voice! Don't just pick ANY pivotal moment.

TEMPLATE:

Real talk: there have been numerous times in my life when I've gone with my gut , even when it wasn't the easy route. Times when folk questioned my logic, times when family members laid claim to caution, times when others told me I would fail.

Was it scary? Yes. Hard? Yes, especially during these 3 life-changing events:

Starting from ZERO is so hard. And this is why I promised that I was going to help at least 1,000 people who are struggling with _____ .

That's the WHY behind my _____ program.

If you're _____ (describe their challenge), just know that my mission-driven invitation is OPEN and waiting for you.

Your dreams are calling. Would you say yes?

Week 40

Imagine Your Life 6 Months from Now... Where Do You Want It to Be? What Are You Doing? Who Are You With?

STRATEGY:

Engage with your fans. This will have an amazing visual of a place you want to be.

TEMPLATE:

A magical view in one of Palawan's most beautiful lagoons, the famous Twin Lagoons will always stand out as one of the best places to visit in the Philippines.

I haven't seen anything more beautiful and impressive than these lagoons and I want to go back, but not alone.

I would love to host a retreat here, with amazing _____. So, Universe, please take note!

How about you? Where do you want to be in 6 months?

I Want to Give More

STRATEGY:

Success comes from giving and elevating people. Let's offer them some access to you.

TEMPLATE:

Are you setting a personal challenge every month? Have you been checking in on your progress? Even now, you can set a goal for yourself that excites you and brings you joy. It could be as simple as reading a book a week or trying a new recipe.

What is your goal this month? 👇

I am writing each response and will make sure to make myself accountable to help you achieve YOUR goal!

Ready?

Love Note

STRATEGY:

Share a picture of a review. Optional: call your clients by your branded unique name. Be consistent with your brand voice. You don't need to use the word "love".

TEMPLATE:

Check out another great review from a very happy Goddess Unique supporter.

We told you our products work. If you haven't placed your order from Goddess Unique yet you are truly missing out.

Ask The Experts Series Part 1 - Video or Written

STRATEGY:

Think about your niche and your voice! Don't just pick ANY question. If you need ideas for questions, you can use Google Trends to see what people are searching for.

TEMPLATE:

This week we have a series of topics lined up for you! Head over to our website to learn more about them and get the chance to submit your question!

(Link in BIO)

*This post is assuming that you will add a specific link where your fans can submit their questions.

*If you don't have landing pages, use Google Form. Then, connect your form link to Linktr.ee.

Ask the Experts Series Part 2

STRATEGY:

Rally your fans letting them know the topics that they will be watching or reading.

TEMPLATE:

Remember! This week we have a series of topics lined up for you!

Head over to our website to learn more about them and get the chance to submit your question!

(Share an intro about the content so they are motivated to engage.)

Ask The Experts Series Part 3

STRATEGY:

Rally your fans letting them know the topics that they will be watching or reading. Be consistent here.

TEMPLATE:

Have you ever wondered how to _____. If so, then to-day's "Q&A with___" has your name on it! Check this out ____ (where the content is) and come back with your questions!

The Mantra I Repeat to Myself When Things Get Tough/ or My Favorite Song

STRATEGY:

The idea is to ignite conversations. Remember to use your voice and niche.

TEMPLATE:

Love this song! Makes me just sing it out loud!

"I got the eye of the tiger, a fighter

Dancing through the fire

'Cause I am a champion, and you're gonna hear me roar

Louder, louder than a lion

'Cause I am a champion, and you're gonna hear me roar!"

Birthday Is Coming

STRATEGY:

Not sure when is your BD but.... Tell your fans when it is! Make them feel like friends.

Use #birthdaymonth

TEMPLATE:

I am so happy to turn 39 🐢 This year will be my golden year.

This year is different and is totally fine.

Differences are always good.

Any tips from my 40-up friends?

The I Am Thankful
Strategy

Your clients are sending you thank you notes. Can you share a screenshot of their message?

TEMPLATE:

This never gets old. My clients are family!

Week 43

Morning Routine

STRATEGY:

Share your habits of success.

TEMPLATE:

Stretching in the morning routine helps to energize you for the day 🤸 I've been doing it for years!

The feeling of a good stretch in the morning is amazing😍 Along with some yawning!

Happy _____!

Hang Out on IGTV

STRATEGY:

Leverage videos to connect better with your audience.

TEMPLATE:

A few weeks ago, we had such an amazing turn out with great questions!

I have decided to do more IG LIVES to give you all the answers you need to help keep you motivated in your creativity, business, and lives. 🎬

.

.

This week we will be going over: .

.

♀ *Being the FACE of your Brand*

♀ *Why It's important to Niche Your Style Down*

♀ *3 Ways to Ultimately Achieve Big Goals*

Direct Pitch (One offer)

STRATEGY:

Objective: leads and sales

TEMPLATE:

Are you ready to _____? It can transform your business AND your life! 😎

What if you had a TRAINER to navigate you through the details and strategy of implementing your very own customized 30 day plan, so that you knew exactly what to do (AND how to do it) every single day?!

Well, YOU CAN!

Join my _____. Check Link in BIO.

Vacations Ahead

STRATEGY:

Try to get conversations. Ask for ideas.

TEMPLATE:

Prepare a collage with 4 options and ask:

"So... 1,2,3,4, can you give me your reviews?"

A Common Struggle ___ Face

STRATEGY:

Showcase your expertise.

TEMPLATE:

Struggling to create enticing and exciting content?

If so, here's my first tip

**Create an attention-grabbing headline.

**A headline determines if people will read your content.

**If your headline doesn't spark curiosity or even evoke an emotion, then the reader won't want to read more. Which means your content won't get the returns you want.

Need help with creating captivating headlines?

Why I Don't Offer Free ____

STRATEGY:

Reveal a strategy that has helped you get more clients.

TEMPLATE:

When I first started my practice, I used to offer free consultations every Wednesday. I would book calls and give my advice for free.

After almost a year of offering free consulting, I realized that I was not serving my clients. I was doing a disservice to my mission.

Time never comes back. The time I invested in all the free consultations I could have used it to create amazing content and share GLOBALLY and impact MILLIONS.

Once I shifted my mindset around "free-everything", I was able to attract bigger and better opportunities. You see, money is energy. It starts with your mindset.

This is one of my favorite breakthroughs to teach.

Check out my website - Free Resources!

Week 45

What Books Have You Read This Year?

STRATEGY:

This post is a conversation Starter.

TEMPLATE:

Two great reads this week while I'm cooking/doing laundry/packing. Both are research for a new book I'm halfway through writing and a new course I've been brainstorming for weeks. 🎉

"Scientifically, there is no such thing as an average brain." — Scientist Todd Rose.

Wonder why America is still using averages in our education system?!? (Thanks for this amazing book rec, my friend @_____.

Keep Digging for Conversions!

STRATEGY:

Keep following up with those who are on the fence.

TEMPLATE:

There I was on my 8th hour of making just ONE video, even before releasing and promoting it. My content creation process was taking hours away from my business. And the worst part? I wasn't seeing any ROI to make it worth the long hours.

When this continued to happen week after week, I realized that the problem wasn't that I wasn't good at creating content or value. 🔲

🔲

It's because I wasn't crystal clear on my offer and I didn't dial in on the audience that I wanted to attract.

When I figured this out, making impact and profit became much easier because I knew exactly who I was talking to.

Today, I help my clients get crystal clear on their offer and their process to turn their audience into paying customers.

The transformation that my students experience is inspiring. They went from:

"I don't know what to talk about in my videos." → *"Talking is easy for me because I know exactly who I'm speaking to."*

How can you start?

Get my Thought Leader Roadmap that will cut your content creation process in half.

You won't be disappointed!

What Is Success for You?

STRATEGY:

Get your audience to move towards consideration.

TEMPLATE:

There's a lot of talk about defining what success looks like because everyone's version of success is so different.

I measure success by freedom and impact, more so than the **dollar** *figures. I could have a 7-figure business but if I'm not making an impact and I don't feel freedom in my heart and soul, that's not success in my eyes.*

When you see people in your industry accomplishing x,y,z, it can be easy to get swayed into the promise of 'success'.

It's natural to compare yourself to your competition and work for what they have.

But if your goals are based on what someone else has accomplished, then you'll never truly reach a point where you feel fulfilled..

Prioritizing what's important to YOU is the "secret" to success.

Knowing what's in your heart, chasing after it, and ignoring the rest is the true road to victory.

One great way to unlock what success looks like for you is by reflecting on this question:

"What does your dream life look like 30 years from now?"

Get laser-focused on that picture in your head and work relentlessly for it.

Need help? I'm here for you!

Week 46

Welcome New Month

STRATEGY:

This is a conversation starter. You want to share about you, but also make them join the conversation.

Webinar Invite

STRATEGY:

This post is to ignite consideration.

TEMPLATE:

From Blah to Wow - (Webinar)

Do you want to learn how I create 6 Months Of Content in just 3 Days?

And learn about.....

�֎ My Underground Charisma Formula that Celebrities and Top Influencers Use to Look and Feel Amazing on Camera.

✖ My 7 Step Content Machine Process that Brings In Thousands of Leads Every Month in Just 20 Minutes a Day.

� The Exact Technique High Performing Entrepreneurs Use to Out-Earn Top Influencers With Only a Fraction of the Views ᵎ

Then you need to go Register right NOW!

Tonight is your last chance to take advantage of this training packed full of amazing information... if you couldn't already tell. ᵎ

ᵎ

It goes live TONIGHT _____ .

A Big Problem that I Can Solve Today

STRATEGY:

Move your fans to know why they need you today.

TEMPLATE:

If you don't know the theme of your content, you don't know your problem. And if you don't know your problem, you sure as heck are not going to be able to solve it for people.

What is your message about? What is the theme that runs through everything you put out? When you're able to define the problem, you're halfway to the solution.

In my ___ course, I cover step-by-step how you can not only find the problem for your audience but how you might be able to solve it!

Click on the link in my bio to learn more!

Week 47

Motivational Post

STRATEGY:

Ignite likes and conversations.

TEMPLATE:

Don't be afraid to surround yourself with people who are doing much better than you, because they can push you to discover your true potential💪

[;]

Strategic Question

STRATEGY:

Get your audience to consider working with you.

TEMPLATE:

Question: How many books have been given to you that you've never read? It makes you feel guilty, doesn't it? [;]
[;]

[;]

But it shouldn't, because a certain amount of this choice is psychological. We're hardwired this way. When people pay for something, they pay more attention to it. If you get it for free, you don't have that extra incentive to participate in it. [;]

[;]

Plus, the people receiving the payment want to reward you for paying more. They want to give you more value and more access, because you are further along in the subscriber-to-buyer spectrum. Transformation occurs in the transaction. ⊡⊡

⊡⊡

Don't miss out on today's Facebook live where I share more details on how you can do this in your business! ⊡⊡

⊡⊡

⊡

I also highly suggest that you check out the (sales page) - it will (transform/change/give you?)

Selling Your Event/Course

STRATEGY:

Promote an invitation so your audience takes action.

TEMPLATE:

There is a reason for your life.

You were made on purpose, for a purpose, with a very big purpose.

You are here to create a much bigger impact through your business than you are currently doing.

You are meant to experience so much more abundance in your life.

You were meant to play so much bigger in your business than you're playing now.

Yes...even in these uncertain times.

ESPECIALLY when (describe challenges)

But... When your mindset is not yet where it needs to be, you unknowingly get on your own way. It doesn't happen, and you get stuck at the same income level and same impact for YEARS.

The ____ Retreat t is where your big impact (and high quality of life) become your reality by removing your biggest obstacles.

This (details about the experience)

Registration officially closes tomorrow. Come and explore our ticket options (link in bio).

It's Time to Prepare for the Holiday Season!

Strategy

It's the season of joy. Make your audience feel like family.

Template

Christmas Homies!

Even the Railing Needs Decorating 😊

Holidays Decor

Strategy

It's the season of joy. It's the season of joy! Make your audience feel like family.

Template

It's beginning to look a lot like …. is that a pig in a Santa suit? ⛄ 🎄

My Tina Lee inspired pic.

Each December in _____, a bunch of houses put up as many lights as they can!

There were many close contenders, but I think this house won for me.

Do you decorate for the holidays?

Announce Your Upcoming Sale

STRATEGY:

It's the season of joy, enjoy!

TEMPLATE:

We'll see you guys a little later this evening for our special Holiday/Christmas sale at 8:30PM EST!

Countdown to Your Favorite Holiday...

STRATEGY:

It's the season of joy, enjoy!

TEMPLATE:

22 days left 🎄

Cheer Your Team

STRATEGY:

It's the season of joy, enjoy!

TEMPLATE:

Teams who work together, shop together, and have fun together 😍

Holiday Sale

STRATEGY:

You can announce your sale as an ongoing event.

TEMPLATE:

Our Holiday sale is here and we are here to be your one-stop shop for all the amazing gifts!

Stay tuned, because every _____ we will announce our deal of the week!

First _____ will be tomorrow!

Family Pics

STRATEGY:

Ignite your connections.

TEMPLATE:

Behind every small business is a family.

SO— many of you may not realize this- but (share your business success story).

Anyways—behind my small business is the family you see pictured. This family has supported my dream since the very beginning!

I've been thinking a lot lately about everything that it takes to actually run my small business on the daily— and I can't help but realize that I wouldn't be able to "Just BE Jessica" without THEM. I mean- after all, I really don't think anyone else would go along with all of my crazy ideas. Ha.

Are you a small business owner? Is your business a "family affair"? Drop your small business name below!

Enjoying Vacations/ Food?

STRATEGY:

Inspire your audience.

TEMPLATE:

And I am off for winter break, right before a crazy wedding season; so excited about what's to come but first things first, I need to refuel and take some me-time; follow along my trip on stories ... you take care ;)

Deal of the Week

STRATEGY:

You can announce your sale as an ongoing event.

TEMPLATE:

DEAL OF THE WEEK: This week only, use code SAVE____ to get $10 OFF our popular_____.

Tag a friend who needs this today!

Week 51

Favorite Recipe (Cookies)

STRATEGY:

Ignite conversations!

TEMPLATE:

I had too much fun in the planning process for all of these
_____ cookies 😂

How Do I Make Money?

STRATEGY:

This is a catchy question. You will get your users to think about value instead of money.

TEMPLATE:

"How do I make more money?" 💰

This is probably one of the most common questions people ask me. Here's what I tell them in my seminars, calls, and books.

The start of this entire process is to ask the right question.

And "How do I make more money?" is not that question.

No matter what industry you're in, some of the questions you should be asking are...

... How can I add more value?

... How can I help more people?

The truth is, money is just a result ✅

Money is a byproduct of helping somebody else.

Whether it's for my company, personal brand or going into a foreign market, I always start the process by thinking about...

... what are these people struggling with?

If you're thinking about goals, I hope this makes you define new goals.

Deal Of The Week

STRATEGY:

You can announce your sale as an ongoing event.

TEMPLATE:

DEAL OF THE WEEK: This week only, use code SAVE_____ to get $10 OFF our popular_____.

Tag a friend who needs this today!

Week 52

Pet Picture!

STRATEGY:

Ignite conversations!

TEMPLATE:

Fashionable lady here 😎 Wishing you a happy holiday!

Deal of the Week

STRATEGY:

You can announce your sale as an ongoing event.

TEMPLATE:

DEAL OF THE WEEK: This week only, use code SAVE____ to get $10 OFF our popular_____.

Tag a friend who needs this today!

Ringing the New Year

STRATEGY:

Ignite conversations!

TEMPLATE:

Are you ready to ring in ____? 🎉 Still cannot believe the year is ending but looking forward to what the new year has in store. What are your goals and resolutions? Hope it brings us more joy and happiness, and all about the good vibes!!! ♥

(Share one audacious goal with your audience!)

PART 5:

Social Visibility

After leaving 52 weeks of content, I cannot wrap this book up without talking about hashtags and other aspects that will significantly impact your visibility.

How to Measure Visibility From Your Social Media Channels? What's Best to Track?

Have you heard people saying that organic social media is dead? What exactly do they mean? Organic social media refers to how many people will see your content without having to pay for advertising.

Using common sense, you will think that visibility is a metric on each platform. Well, it is not. There are two common metrics that you will see: reach and impressions. It is important to understand what they mean.

Reach and impressions refer to two distinct activities.

Reach refers to the total number of people who have seen your ad or content. If 100 total people have seen your ad, that means your ad's reach is 100.

Impressions refer to the number of times your ad or content has been displayed on a screen. Let's say that your ad from the previous example popped up on those people's screens a total of 300 times. That means the number of impressions for that ad is 300.

Reach and impressions are both important metrics. If you are not seeing good impressions, this is a reflection of the quality of your content. Perhaps the visuals are not adequate, the algorithm is getting negative feedback, or your hashtags are being banned.

If you are not seeing good reach, this means that your account needs to grow the audience. Therefore, you might want to pay for advertising to just get more reach.

Now that you know which metrics matter, you will monitor your reach and impressions at least once a month.

Let's take a look at hashtags since it is another popular area where you can apply technical visibility strategies.

How Do You Use Hashtags on Instagram?

Are you wondering how exactly you can find the gold of Instagram Hashtags that everyone talks about? Are you confused about how many hashtags you should use on Instagram?

Some marketers say it is 30, but others say to not do it because it's spammy. This is very confusing, especially because they do not give you a logical reason.

Spoiler alert! My Instagram Hashtags Cheat Sheet is coming your way. But... numbers truly do not matter, unless you are using each hashtag with a specific strategy in mind.

Do not feel bad if you don't know exactly what a hashtag is. This is one of the most asked questions during my social media workshops and webinars.

In information systems, a tag is a keyword or term assigned to a piece of information (such as an Internet bookmark, digital image, database record, or computer file). This kind of metadata helps describe an item and allows it to be found again by browsing or searching.

A hashtag is a type of metadata tag. Ok.... That didn't seem too basic...

From a user standpoint, hashtags are used to categorize content, making the new or related articles and insights easy to find.

Every time a post has a hashtag at the caption or on the first comment, it will be added to a tag category that makes people find your post.

Important note: your posts will only be visible in public walls if your profile is public.

Four Most Important Elements of Your Instagram Hashtag Strategy to Get Followers in 2020

1. Who do you want to attract?
2. WITFM (what's in there for me). What will be the one thing that your users will stop at your account, follow you, and come for more?
3. Metrics and benchmarks so you have a GPS to track your route to success

4. Amazing content, not just based on what you think but based on your metrics

Instagram Hashtag Search

What many Instagram marketers seem to miss is that search engine marketing is applicable to Instagram.

Search engine marketing (SEM) is a digital marketing strategy used to increase the visibility of a website, or a social media channel in this case.

I know what you are thinking: Can I really employ the same SEO techniques I use to optimize web pages for a social media app?

Fortunately, you can.

The trick is not shoe-horning Instagram into your existing SEO strategy, but rather to use what you already know about SEO to drive organic growth to your Instagram account.

Think of Instagram as its own search engine. The platform has built-in search functions that act as its own mini-Google.

You can search and see Instagram search trends. If you are familiar with SEO and Local SEO, you can also use locations to see the top posts and quickly identify a strategy to climb up there!

For now, even if you are not a digital marketing expert in SEO, just know that you can use the search bar to see the popularity of a hashtag.

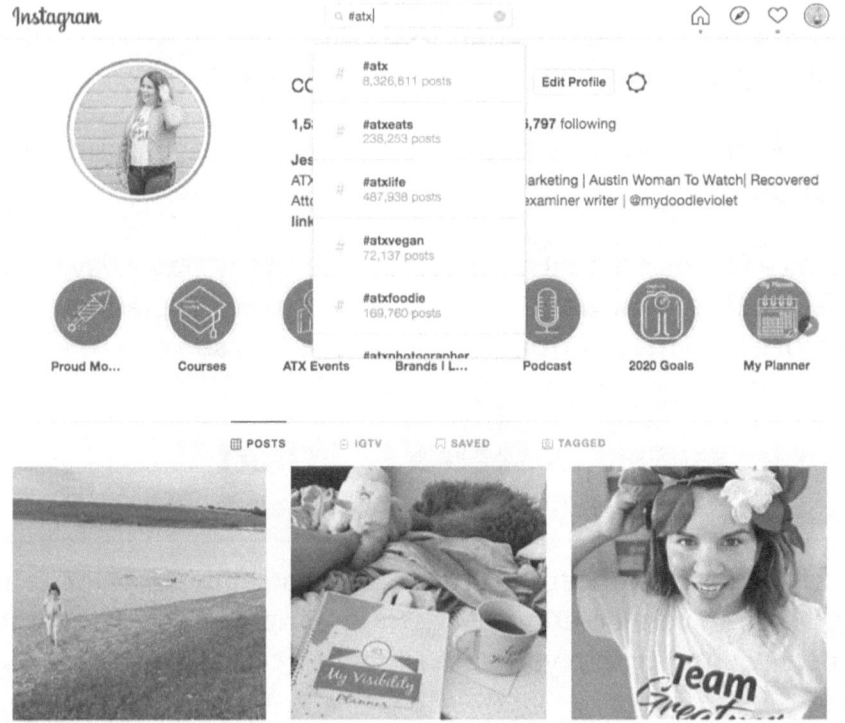

Instagram Hashtags for Likes

Who doesn't want to feel like the Kardashians? I mean, hello! We all want to reach that level of visibility ... but... What is the point behind showing likes? Read this again.

You certainly can explore what are the top hashtags using a tool like All-Hashtag.com and get ideas to get more likes, but you need to be careful in the application of those hashtags.

Adding a # on a post means that your picture will be visible on that # wall. You better watch what else is there before using those #'s with millions of images.

When hashtags are used incorrectly, people looking for new content have to dig through irrelevant, miscategorized content to get to what they're actually looking for.

You do not want this bad user experience associated with your brand!

So, as a forensic digital marketing expert, I say stay away from this practice. You want to see your very own # planner and explore how they perform. I will discuss this so keep reading!

Top Instagram Hashtags to Attract Real Instagram Followers

Hashtags are supposed to help users to search specific topics and join conversations. When done right, a good hashtag strategy should help you get visible in front of your ideal users.

Be strategic. Take some time to think about your imaginary buyer.

1. Interests
2. Journey
3. Vibe
4. Location
5. Associations
6. Influence

Attract Users Who Are Ready to Buy

Instagram is not Amazon. Users are not there with their credit cards ready to buy.

If you are not getting users who are ready to buy, maybe you are reaching users who are not ready for you.

Instagram has users ready to buy! But remember, it is not like Amazon. They do not have a credit card in hand and are actively searching for a product or a service.

But...

Great news! More than one in ten users are using the platform specifically to shop or find new products.

Your future best client is active on Instagram and, yes, could buy from you!

Maybe they are searching for ideas and find your picture. If they stop and click on it, they will come to your profile. That is a conversion! Of course, you do not see this activity unless they hit like, comment, or follow you, which might not happen for about 50% of people.

Once they see you, the ball is on your court!

The Seductive Instagram Marketing Funnel

The game is on.

When users are on your page, your goal is to captivate their attention and show them your value in less than five seconds.

Do you think your Instagram page can do that? Be honest.

The seductive Instagram Marketing Funnel starts with your strategic thinking!

As a forensic digital marketer, I always advise marketers to design their social media channels using Information Architecture Principles.

Never take a digital marketing plan from anyone. As a business owner, you know your audience best.

How to Turn Users Into Customers

Remember, Instagram users are mostly searching. They are on top of your funnel. Your goal is to lead them as close to you as you can.

Direct messages are a great option, especially when you are starting. Therefore, get used to having real conversations with your users and invite them for a call.

Collaborate with Other Brands for More Visibility

In our case, we also collaborated with Vcita.com to help them spread awareness about the COVID experience, so that worked very well with our Visibility Planner campaign.

How Many Hashtags on Instagram

You definitely want to attract as many users as possible to your *Seductive Instagram Marketing Funnel.*

You will be using 30 hashtags. Why? Because ... why not?

The caveat here is how will you turn this magical number into deposits on your banking account.

We recommend dividing them into 6 categories.

1. Your expertise: *what kind of expert would your imaginary user listen to?*

2. Your segment or niche: *think about how those users who are actively considering*

3. Your brand voice: *what would get users to join a conversation?*

4. Your content: *description of your picture.*

5. Your location: *your city or place where you want to do business.*

6. What's today: *leave room for spontaneity!*

Pick five of each category so you can get the 30 hashtags.

Note: This book comes with a Workbook where you can plan your hashtags as well!

Facebook & Instagram Ads

Once you implement a robust content marketing plan and you feel like your brand is on point and your social media channels are in a good rhythm, maybe it is time to explore Facebook & Instagram ads.

How to Craft a Winning Targeting Strategy

Audience targeting is one of the most fascinating features that Facebook offers.

Where to start?

A great place to start gathering intelligence about your target audience is on Facebook Audience Insights. You will be able to see details about your audience that are beyond demographics, like digital behavior for example. This means that Facebook already knows what kind of content and especially what kind of ads will most likely appeal to your audience.

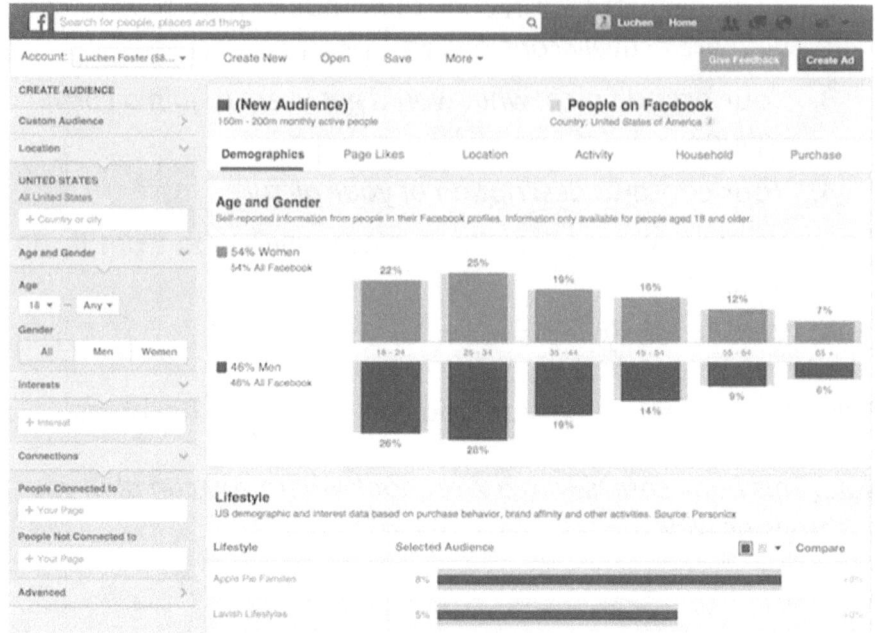

From Audience Insights you can also save your audience. Just make sure this audience is saved on your correct Facebook Ads account.

If you are not sure, just use the data from Audience Insights and create a new audience from your business manager.

On Business Manager menu, go to Assets- Audiences

Once you are on the Audiences dashboard, select "create a saved audience".

This is the process to create a new audience, which we recommend to craft a fresh campaign. Try to have an audience just under 1M users. This will be relevant when it comes to selecting your budget.

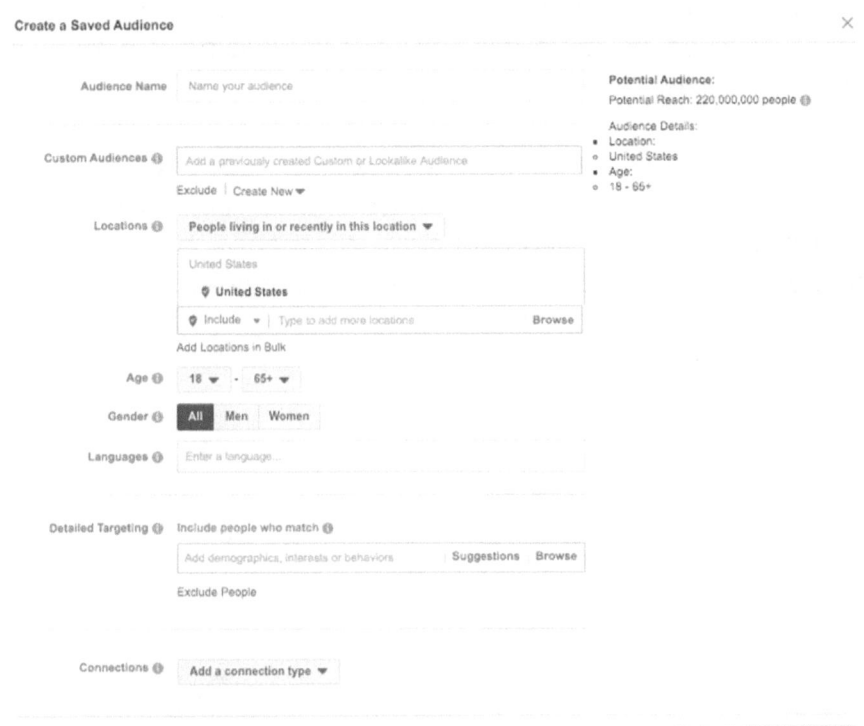

Ads Budget Calculator

When it comes to budget, we like to suggest a formula based on the estimated daily reach and estimated conversion rates.

Facebook has reported that its optimization phase starts after 10,000 views in a 30-day period.

What does this mean?

It means that your goal is to get 10,000 users coming to your point of conversions (sales page, lead page, etc.). Once this number has been reached, the platform starts to optimize itself to achieve the campaign goals.

Here's a way to strategize your 10,000 benchmark in a 30-day window: 300,000 accounts reached with a 3% CTR = 10,000 views (tracked as "pixel fires"). How can we do it within 30 days? Choosing the right budget!

Look, for example, a campaign with $20 a day for 30 days. This has an estimated reach of 1,800 to 5,100. If we hit the best-case scenario, (5,100 per day), this means that in 30 days we have 153,000. But... that is not the benchmark!

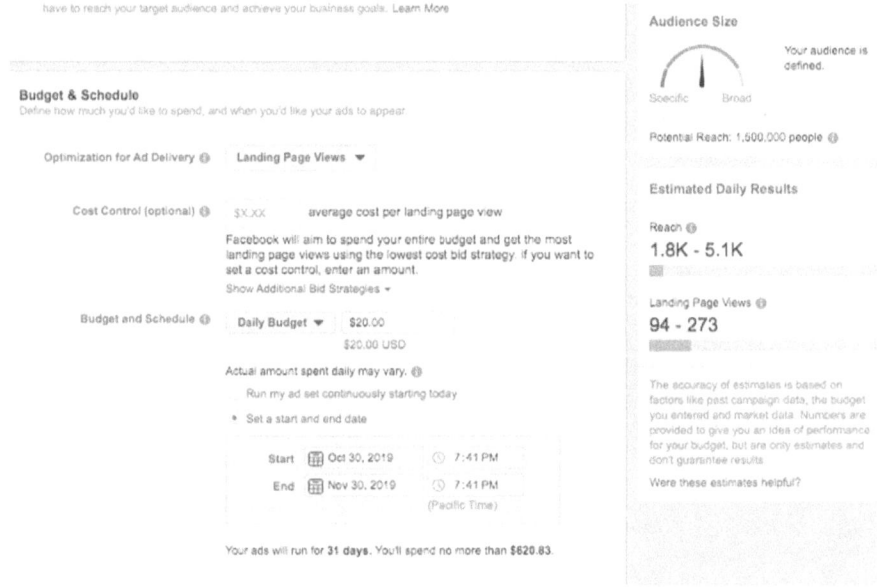

Let's see the same campaign, with a daily $100 budget. Best case scenario went 4x higher. 22,000 a day. That is a reach of 660,000 accounts. But remember, that is your best-case scenario.

What budget should you use then?

Start this campaign with $100 a day. You will have much quicker results (and better). You can always adjust the budget during your campaign.

For example, set up a campaign for week 1, $100 a day, then monitor results for the next 3-5 days.

Week 2, $80 a day and monitor the results.

Remember, this testimonial ad will also be placed on your business page and will reach people organically as well.

Do not be afraid of adding a reasonable budget to your campaign. Playing with $5 a day "to see what happens" will not give you the best results. Facebook has ways to deliver you the best results possible, with their campaign budget optimization feature.

A note on the pixel fires: For the purpose of 10,000 pixel fires, every website traffic source matters. In other words, if you are blogging and using SEO, those visitors count towards the 10,000 goal. Blogging is good!

Since you have the content and ways to promote your content, now the next question will be how to know what is working from all your digital marketing activities.

This is my area of expertise! It is Forensic Marketing.

Social Visibility Formula

By now you should have memorized what does visibility mean! Can you think about this for just a moment? Let me give you a simple formula:

Right Message + Target Audience = Visibility

When you have a conversation with someone who is interested in your product or services, that's visibility.

We use social media marketing and other digital marketing channels to expand that visibility. But we cannot forget offline channels!

Ideas for offline marketing:

- Promotional products
- Business cards
- Trade shows
- Speaking at events
- Networking events
- Press releases
- Workshops
- Direct mail
- Coupons
- Flyers
- Cold calling

Your Visibility Baseline

I am sure you have some connections. Your cellphone contacts, LinkedIn connections, Facebook friends, email list. That is your baseline. When I do this exercise at the workshops, I usually ask people to try to guess the number of contacts they have. Then I ask them to check for each of those channels. Very often, I hear "wow, I had no idea"! You might be surprised at how many contacts you already have. So, I encourage you to take the time and calculate your baseline.

- ◆ Contacts on cellphone   _____
- ◆ LinkedIn connections   _____
- ◆ Facebook friends   _____
- ◆ Facebook acquaintances   _____
- ◆ Instagram close friends   _____
- ◆ Neighbors   _____
- ◆ Associations (BNI, etc.)   _____
- ◆ Close circle of friends   _____
- ◆ Influencers   _____

Now add the numbers and this is your baseline.

The next step is to check out your brand position in Google. Notice that I am not asking for likes, shares or comments on social media. The reason is because engagement in social media is part of your marketing process, but it is not a relevant metric when it comes to growing your brand.

Most marketers call likes and shares "vanity metrics" and I tend to agree. You cannot deposit likes into your banking account.

Your brand visibility is measured at your website level unless you are a physical location, which includes foot traffic.

If you have a website, you should see the number of users and searches that are happening. Not sure? Then, check out Google Search Console- a free and powerful tool that will reveal plenty of information about how people are finding you on Google.

Are you worried that you are in ground zero? It's ok. We all need to start at zero. The key is to have a path to reach the visibility that your brand needs so you can start generating sales!

Your Path to Social Visibility

It takes a village to lift a brand from ground zero! But the key here is to be strategic, or else you will suffer from marketing burn. Your brain will be full of ideas. You will have a pile of unfinished projects and nothing will get done.

Social media marketing has a lot to offer when it comes to reaching visibility. First of all, it's free. Second, each platform provides free training for those who are interested in learning how to use it for business.

If social media channels are free and business owners can learn how to be successful at no charge, why does it feel so complicated? If it feels complicated, it is because there is no strategy. As a result:

- ◆ Your expectations from social media marketing could be wrong.
- ◆ You might not have a plan of action.
- ◆ It is hard to be consistent.
- ◆ It will feel like you are throwing spaghetti at the walls to see what sticks.

What if you detach yourself from the pressure of seeing sales happening on social media and instead put all your energy to connect with people as humans?

By using the power of word of mouth, you will be expanding your network in no time, and inevitably your business will gain visibility.

Social Visibility

Focus in marketing **experiences**.

A satisfied individual will tell 2-3 people about his **experience** with your company.

If each of them share on social media, on average, they can reach 1,000 people. That's 2,000 new people exposed to your business, in just one message!

2,000 x 365= 730,000 organic potential reach in a year, FREE. If this formula fails by 99%, that is still 7,300 people!

When you start making real connections, you leave an indelible impression on your audience. At this point, people will research you. People will want to know more about you, what you do, your story and who you are connected to. This is because **First Impressions Last**.

After listening to what you have to say, your background and history as well as what you are currently doing will be the core interest of your audience. This is because people want to be able to identify with you or be inspired and motivated. Therefore, branding is very important. You must represent your message well. When a prospect visits your social media handles, what they see must coincide with and enhance your message.

Even though there are billions of people on Facebook, Instagram, LinkedIn and all the other social media platforms, there is still room for you to stand out from the crowd. You need to find a way to come out as someone unique and someone who really offers value to your market so people are eager to find out what it is that you do, and why they should hire you as opposed to your competitors. This is the reason why you need to spruce your profile.

Facebook Profile Checklist

For Facebook, you may take these simple steps to upgrade your account to better connect with people and leave a lasting impression.

Profile Picture: Invest in your profile picture. A selfie is unacceptable. Give yourself a lift in order to stand out from the crowd. Set up a session with your photographer and have professional photos taken for your profile picture.

Cover Picture: Your cover picture should align with your values, brand, and vision

About Section: Your "About" section should not be private. Strangers should be able to see who you are and be able to find you.

Tag Line: Facebook gives you the tag line for free. You may add one or two sentences up to 150 characters here. Take advantage of this opportunity and add one or two sentences about yourself.

Life Moments: All your connections will be able to view every time you update your "life moment." Take advantage of receiving free promotion and utilize this feature.

Notes: For those who are interested in blogging, the notes are opportunities to write blog articles and blog posts. Blogging is an excellent marketing activity to drive traffic to your page.

Privacy: Learn how to adjust your privacy settings. You should be able to control who posts on your timeline, whether you accept those posts or reject them. Also, it is important that you limit the visibility of your connections. You are the only person who should be seeing the names of your friends. This is something you really want to do. Another feature that is important under the privacy tab is checking exactly who can find you. Do not limit this feature because you want strangers to be able to find you.

Albums: The photo albums are an opportunity to let the world know who you are. Create a set of at least 6 albums with photos that reflect your vision, mission, products, opportunities and family so that people can get balanced information about who you are.

When taking photos, you should always have the Dress to Impress principle in mind: When you are receiving strangers to your profile, it is important that your photos reflect the best version of you. You need to dress to impress!

The secret to connecting with others is to nurture relationships. When you make branding a priority, and you master how to brand your marketing message, you never have to sell! At this point in your business, people will pursue you instead of you pursuing them!

Farmer vs Hunter in Social Media

In sales, people often refer to 2 types of salespeople, farmers and hunters. I believe that we can apply similar principles in social selling.

Before even meeting a person, think about how you can help the person. If someone shows interest in your business, do some research on the person. Find out what they are into, their likes and dislikes, etc. After gathering your information, ask yourself, how can I help this person outside of their specific interest in my business? Offer that little extra. Remember, it is the little things that we do that we are remembered for. **Try to offer more value than you are paid for**. End your conversations by committing to help. Follow up and deliver on your commitments. Practice with as many people as possible.

Social Selling Is All About Value

Imagine this scenario: a coworker invited you for a family party. You know a few of the other coworkers, but everyone else is a stranger. How do you approach people at the party? Do you stop them, get on their face, and tell them to buy from you? Of course not. You would get to know them first, ask questions, engage in conversations to find things in common.

Adding value is not subject to your opinion. Your users will find value depending on their very own stage. This is what makes marketing a very complex process.

How Do You Track Your Success From Social Media Marketing When You Are Using a Social Selling Approach?

This is a great question. In fact, I just got off the phone with April, a Yoga studio owner in Louisiana. She asked: "I can measure how many customers sign up versus how many people come through the door, but how can I see this in social media, can we track? My response: we will track! But your best indication is when you start getting messages from people asking for information about your services.

Your best indicator of your social selling success is when you start getting referrals from the platform itself, or from people. This is a great benchmark that you should celebrate!

How can you speed up getting referrals?

Giving referrals first! That is the simplest answer. The more you give, the more you get.

Building a Sales Funnel

Social media is not just about selfies. Of course, we will strategize to attract sales. However, it might not look like "buy from me, I have 50% off today". It is not transactional as Amazon or eBay.

This conversation takes us to discuss *sales funnels*.

During the past few decades, the marketing funnel served as the primary model for how people learn about a product, decide to buy, and (hopefully) become loyal customers, helping spread the word to others.

In today's age when every product has hordes of competitors, the loyalty loop is a more accurate picture of how the customer reevaluates their decision to buy again and again.

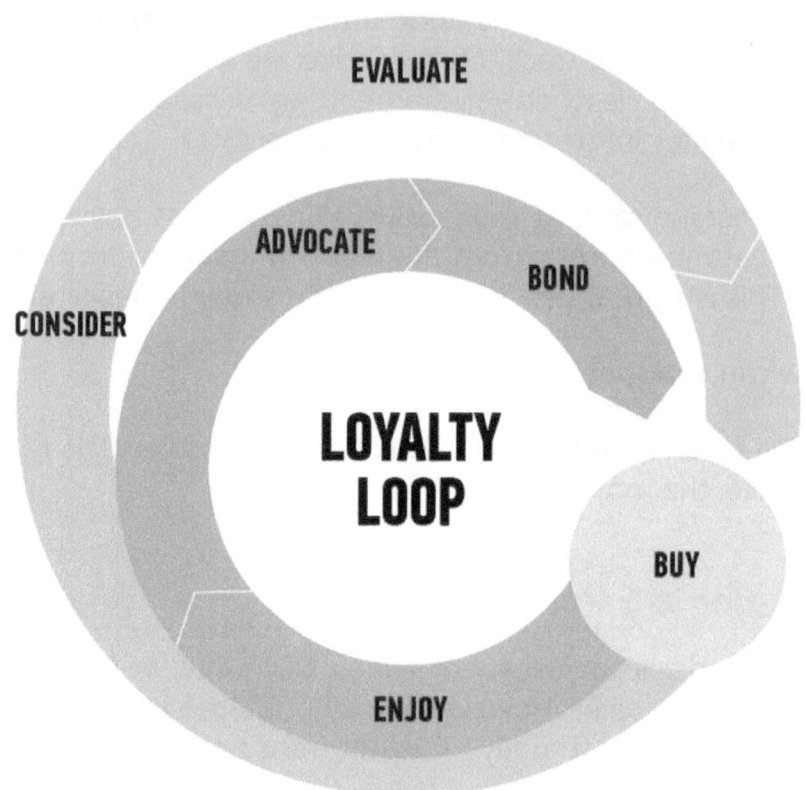

EVALUATE

ADVOCATE

BOND

CONSIDER

LOYALTY LOOP

BUY

ENJOY

The best way to connect with your audience on Facebook or any other social channel is by mapping their experience, all while considering each stage of their decision-making process.

Gone are the days when professionals keep their professional and personal accounts separated. People buy you! Entrepreneurs who are able to build a personal brand thrive in social media. Remember, 76% of buyers are ready to have a social media conversation with potential providers.

Your social media channels are the amplifier. But you need a brand and a voice that speaks to your target audience.

That is where your content marketing strategy comes handy!

Now that you know this, you can go back to the 52 weeks of content that I prepared and notice how much value I am encouraging you to add to your audience. I did not add 52 different ways to "get more sales", on purpose.

My philosophy for success is simple: give people tools to talk about you!

TRACKING YOUR RESULTS- FORENSIC MARKETING

Be honest! You can be writing all day, but you hate numbers! You see your Google Analytics, CTR %'s, Google Search Console reports and ... now what? 😩

Data can come from anywhere. Insights come from intelligence.

What is the first thing that comes to your mind when the word "forensic" is mentioned? Well, most Gen X and millennials associate it with crime investigation. Watch one episode of a crime television show, and you will hear the word forensics mentioned every minute. However, the word has a broader use than you might have imagined.

This is particularly true when it comes to the marketing field. Marketing these days has become a never-ending game of one-upping the competition. Whether it is inbound, outbound, or email marketing, you never know who is going to best you in the days to come.

Because of this uncertainty, people often contemplate giving up. In several cases, people are unable to determine a scalable, steady, predictable and logical path. Lack of clarity drives them insane, which leads them to make wild and risky decisions. Luckily, forensic marketing is there to save the day. In simple words, forensic marketing provides you the cold hard evidence that pinpoints which of your marketing efforts is not working.

However, forensics is not just restricted to marketing or criminology. It is also present in various other fields' like law, medicine and accounting.

Marketing Needs Forensics

Let us briefly discuss the role of forensics in these fields:

Forensic Accounting: This form of forensics helps to find out accounting anomalies in standard practices and records.

Forensic Medicine: helps to point out inconsistencies in medicines and treatments that patients go through. The discrepancies are gauged through patient response.

Forensic Attorneys: The job of a forensic attorney is supporting and concluding court cases by closing the gap between law and science. Attorneys thoroughly go through crime scene evidence that might help them to conclude the situation.

So, have you noticed what forensics in any field have in common? Well, they all help to point out irregularities and inconsistencies. Imagine incorporating forensics for your company's marketing efforts. If done right, the only thing stopping you from achieving your goal would be an act of God.

Is Forensic Marketing a Real Thing?

Forensic marketing is as real as it gets. Think of it as data mining. Tons of companies use data mining to extract useful information out of raw data. They use software that helps them see specific patterns, which offer them a lot of helpful information about customers. It allows businesses to come up with efficient marketing strategies, which decreases their costs and increases their sales. In short, the process of forensic marketing consists of several steps.

Finding the right balance for your marketing strategy is the ultimate goal of forensic marketing. Utilizing forensic marketing will provide you with scalability and predictability that will lead to the massive growth of revenue.

Another aspect of forensic marketing is being aware of the next step that you will take after identifying issues, weaknesses and challenges. If you are unable to rectify a situation, chances are that future outcomes will become even worse. It does not matter whether you are a VP of Marketing or Chief Executive Officer; your ultimate goal should be to identify and fix weaknesses and optimize your client's marketing efforts.

Reviewing your current marketing activities and sales process helps you to make the necessary amendments to achieve your targets.

The World Through a Forensic Microscope

As I discussed earlier, most professional services have a forensic component these days. Be it tax specialists, lawyers, or accountants, you will find some level of forensics in their specialties. Uncovering what has unraveled is the primary purpose of using a forensic approach in marketing. Much like crime scene investigations, the forensic marketing microscope helps to find the culprit behind your company's revenue and leads or lack thereof.

Assessing current marketing through forensics is quite simple. Here is what happens:

Your business (or your client's business) provides a solution for a group of people. That is your target audience. You want to get visible in front of that group, so they know about your solution. But you also want to influence them, so they become your client. This is where forensics comes handy. It is all about turning insights into actionable steps so the business can achieve its goals.

Marketers Have a Hard Time Proving the ROI From Their Digital Marketing Efforts

Most marketers have quite a difficult time when it comes to proving the returns from their digital marketing efforts, be it from content marketing or social media marketing. Being a marketer, I have noticed that we often juggle heaps of projects. So much so, that many marketers find themselves later on in a turbulent whirlwind that never lets them do their jobs properly. The result is the inability to report on ROI of all the marketing responsibilities they take on. Finding accurate data and presenting it becomes increasingly hard.

According to a reputable survey, marketers from various countries were asked what their biggest challenge is when they try to attempt their marketing's ROI. The vast majority of these marketers reported that attributing to their digital marketing ROI was most problematic for them. A significant reason why proving ROI for digital marketing, especially when it comes to content production, is quite tough is because most analytics platforms base their reports by on-page SEO, local SEO, paid searches, email, social media insights, ad performance and other channels. Surprisingly, even sophisticated attribution models do not show whether the money you spent on your marketing efforts was worth it or not.

Despite that, there are a few things you can do to improve your efforts. First, use a top website analytics platform like Google Analytics for reporting your campaigns with accuracy. In addition, use tracking codes for all marketing activities that make use of your content. UTM codes are a good example of that. Furthermore, report your content by using a custom dashboard.

By having these, you will find It easier to report the impact of each of your marketing efforts. It will also help you combine your financial and campaign reports. These challenges can be conquered; However, you have to step back from the production line, find suitable key performance indicators for the business, and use tools that match your needs. Sure, you might find it painstaking in the beginning; However, with time, you will see a significant improvement in proving ROI on your digital activities.

Organizations Want to See Conversion Rates and Real Sales, Not Just Clicks

Conversion rates are, without a doubt, the most crucial digital media and digital marketing metric. All your online marketing efforts, especially content marketing, aim at a single purpose, and that is to convert your website visitors into loyal customers.

Conversion rates include more than just sales. Free quote requests by visitors, calls, and filling contract forms are also considered conversions. Any action that increases the chances of your business making a sale can be referred to as a conversion.

I have seen quite a lot of people become overwhelmed by metrics in their early digital marketing days. You should always watch click-through rates and CPC while keeping return on investment in mind. Do not make the mistake of diverting all your attention to clicks. It is a recipe for disaster. Organizations care more about real sales and conversion rates.

If you have not done it yet, before moving forward with your content marketing plan, tracking your entire sales process is a must. Facebook provides a great feature to track clicks and actions with Pixel Event Setup Tool. You can use it to track your blog and call to actions, for example. This will be the only way for you to show that your content marketing is turning into real users.

Importance of Measuring Conversions From Your Content Marketing

If it is not abundantly clear by now, improving conversion rates is the cheapest possible way to improve profits from your content marketing efforts.

If this was not enough, here are some more reasons that solidify the importance of conversion rates:

Conversion Rates Indicate Failure and Success

As a content marketer, you typically pay attention to keywords, keyword density, and other SEO tools that help you craft the best content marketing strategy. But your work does not end there.

Besides your SEO metrics, a content marketer needs to track their conversion rates from their content marketing efforts. This is the only way you can tell if your content marketing is working.

You Save Money With Better Conversion Rates

Higher conversion rates allow you to cover a lot of ground without having a big ad budget. You can even reduce the current ad budget and use cash leftover to test new marketing tactics. Your banking account will appreciate it.

Conversion Rates Tell You About Your Readability

Readability is a major factor in online content and can greatly increase your site's search engine optimization (SEO) levels. Readability is the practice of making your writing understandable and easy to digest for your target audience. Marketing to your audience is critically important.

If your conversions are healthy, chances are your readability is healthy as well. On the other hand, if conversion rates are not optimal, exploring readability scores is a must.

A common mistake I see is that marketers only track conversions from their sales page. However, they seem to miss other elements that are important to drive conversions for a website, such as brand authority and brand trust. How do we measure those?

Conversion Rates Are Impulsed by Trust

If your audience can relate to the content that you have created, then they are more likely to trust your brand. But that is not enough for them to purchase from you.

"Businesses that fail to establish trust — the foundation of any relationship — will lose to businesses who can," said SurveyMonkey CEO Zander Lurie in a statement accompanying the survey results. The survey conducted by his company found that brand trust affects the bottom line in a variety of ways.

As a forensic marketer, sometimes I need to step back from the quantitative metrics and explore deeper the qualitative ones such as trust, empathy, relatability, approachability and charisma. Maybe your conversions are not happening simply because the brand does not inspire trust to the audience. Or it is not delivering the information that users expect, in comparison to similar products or services.

Tips to Improve Conversion Rates

Since we have discussed why conversions are so important, let us talk about some helpful tips that could potentially boost conversion rates from your content marketing efforts.

- ♦ Be impeccable with your online presence. Users will search you! Grow your company's social media, add a business listing, add it on google maps, provide the necessary email addresses, etc. Do everything possible to attract people to Twitter, Facebook, and other accounts. Display social proof on your pages if you happen to have a decent following. Also, remember to use title tags and meta tags to improve your online presence.

- ♦ Have a clear definition of what is a conversion. Your initial goal from your content marketing is to build awareness. You need to measure your performance based on the number of users your content marketing is attracting. Optimize for traffic, engagement, and email subscribers, until you reach at least 5,000 visitors per month. Then you can optimize for sales.

- ♦ Niche! Although aiming for a wide audience is a great idea, you should also focus on the particular demographic that appreciates your product the most.

This can be confusing but trust me, it takes me seconds to see your blind spots. That is why you want a forensic strategist in your team!

Case Study

There was a local Tech Company that saw a noticeable decline in its sales and leads suddenly. This happened in late June 2019. The company got in touch with its marketing agency and asked what the problem was. The agency did not find any issues and claimed that everything was alright. They said, "all you need is to increase your PPC budget".

Tech Company agrees to boost their PPC budget to $20,000 a month. Guess what happened next? Do you think sales went up?

If your answer was no, you were right!

Things did not improve. In fact, they got even worse. The sales saw a massive 40 percent drop despite adding a lot of extra budget for enhancing the marketing efforts.

This is when they called me on-site to perform a Forensic Analysis for their marketing to figure out the missing pieces. They did know that something was wrong but could not figure out what it was. All their marketing agency provided was invoices and click rates, which are not enough.

Their marketing agency could not provide an explanation of why sales were not happening, simply because they were just doing one tactic: PPC. The center of their tactic was the money factor, instead of the user. But the client is not a marketer, so they do not know what they do not know.

From my analysis, I found critical conversion metrics that were missing- all related to their top-funnel marketing. They had no content marketing strategy in place, except for the product description and call to action. I showed them their top competitors and their content marketing. We drafted a top-funnel content marketing plan that will drive them up to

40,000 new visitors – all organic. By adding organic traffic, their marketing budget went from $25,000 a month to $7,500 but now it includes content marketing, social media marketing, and PPC. We are now monitoring sales patterns so we can craft advertising campaigns, based on what their users want!

Our 6 Steps of Forensic Marketing Consulting

We are highly proficient when it comes to forensic marketing, whether it is for a local business or for a wider one. Our efforts have provided first-rate marketing solutions for various renowned clients. Here are our 6 steps of forensic marketing consultancy.

Before Taking a Case – Assessment

The first thing that we offer is a complimentary marketing health check. I was very adamant of making it part of our assessment because it was a system I had since my law firm days. I do not take cases that are hopeless and unwinnable. It saves time and money for both parties. I have turned down cases numerous times, as I know how much clients appreciate honest pros.

Our forensic consultancy will help you with coming up with a brand development strategy. We use web analytics tools and determine local search ranking, along with other ranking factors to see how far we can take your brand. This will also help you find opportunities to take your optimization to the next level. The form of our one-thousand-dollar worth complimentary assessment will take you 45 seconds to complete. Then on our end, about three hours.

Structure Our Case: Low Hanging Fruits First

After completing our assessment, we come up with a plan of action, along with projected results and budget. The most common deliverables are optimized landing pages, web pages, and competitor keyword analysis. With these, clients see results within a few weeks.

Once the client officially hires us, we then perform deep-dive research to find the areas of opportunities where our clients can see results in the shortest amount of time. This takes about 5 days, and when the client is a marketing agency the process is even faster.

Forensic Audit

It would be fair to say that forensic auditing is probably the most essential part of our job. Our clients provide us with analytics and leave the rest to us. As we always say, data can come from anywhere, insights come from intelligence.

UX Research

We perform a thorough UX research to see whether the online experience you are providing your customers is worthwhile or not. We also conduct UX mapping to improve your digital marketing efforts.

Marketing Strategy

Once we have enough data to establish patterns (30-60 days), we take a holistic strategy for optimal marketing. We then create a marketing calendar with realistic goals in mind. We also make sure that our implementation is bulletproof and free of cracks.

Support (911 Style)

We set up our projects with regular alerts to notify us if there are any errors. We get to work as soon as there is a notification. You can contact us or message us any time you want, as maintaining transparency is of utmost importance to us. It helps to establish trust with customers and improves communication.

COMPLIMENTARY FORENSIC MARKETING SESSION

Since you have invested your precious time to read my book, the least I can do is to invite you for a complimentary discovery session with me.

I would like to know about your business! To claim this gift:

1. Visit my Instagram Page @coachjessicacampos
2. Go to the link in my BIO and select Forensic Marketing Session

Your responses will go straight to my personal email.

I will be delighted to get to know you!

MARKETING GLOSSARY

Buy In: this means people are into doing what you tell them to do.

Buyer's Journey: the process buyers go through to become aware of, consider, evaluate, and decide to purchase a new product or service.

Captions: Depends on the platform. Captions can be another name for the Instagram post. YouTube has open captions and closed captions.

Copy: In advertising, web marketing and similar fields, copy refers to the output of copywriters, who are employed to write material that encourages consumers to buy goods or services.

CTA: Call to action. What you are telling your users you want them to do.

Funnel: The real name is "sales funnel" and it is each step that someone has to take in order to become your customer.

Impressions: Impressions are the number of times your content is displayed, regardless of being clicked or not.

Lead: Individual or organization with an interest in what you are selling.

Prospect: A prospect is a potential customer that you have qualified as fitting certain criteria has shown interest in what you are selling, and there has been a two-way communication. A lead, on the other hand, is one-way communication.

Reach: The total number of different people or households exposed, at least once, to a medium during a given period.

Traffic: It refers to web traffic. The amount of data sent and received by visitors to a website.

UX: User experience is a person's emotions and attitudes about using a particular product, system, or service.

Visibility: Your marketing will generate sales only if you are able to convey your marketing message in front of your ideal audience. And that is what visibility is.

WIFM: What's in it for me?

YOUR GIFT

As a bonus for reading my book, I would like to offer you a free and stylish downloadable planner to help you craft and curate your 52 weeks of social media content.

It truly is plug and play.

To redeem your planner, visit www.visibilitybook.com.

RESOURCES

Besides the books and planners that you can find on Amazon, I have plenty of other resources dedicated to solopreneurs who believe that they were destined to create great things.

Those who own a purpose-driven business.

Those who are called to be industry leaders.

Those who are open to reinvent ... and keep climbing!

If this speaks to you, you will enjoy the rest of my content!

Marketing for Greatness - Facebook Group: this is a space where you can connect with other like-minded individuals. Book readers can ask any questions at any time. Join! Facebook Groups- Marketing for Greatness.

If you have trouble finding it, find Jessica Campos- Marketing for Greatness- Groups

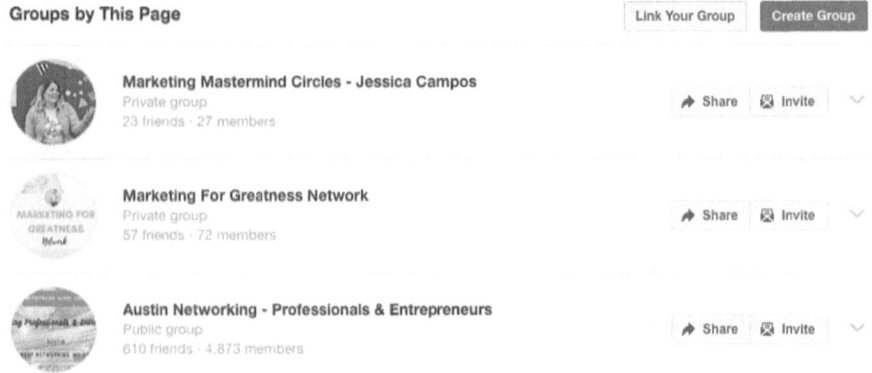

The Visibility Playbook- The Course

This book is jam-packed with information. For some readers, this is enough and you will be well on your way to success. Also, I would imagine that many of you are wanting more.

Great news!

We have a course designed to help you deep dive into the concepts shared in this book and beyond. To learn more visit www.visibilitycourse.com.

The Greatness Blog

I write and teach for a living. This means that you will find a rich blog, full of tips, tutorials, resources, and everything in between.

My blog ideas come from the questions I get during my seminars, webinars, and conversations with business owners like you!

https://www.marketingforgreatness.com/the-greatness-blog/

You can also follow my blog over at *Social Media Examiner.*

https://www.socialmediaexaminer.com/author/jessica-campos/

Marketing For Greatness- The Podcast

The Greatness Podcast is a place where I go when I want to share things on mindset and inspiration.

I am writing a book on personal growth, *Born To be YOUnicorn.* It's a compilation of my life lessons, turned into practical tips to achieve anything in life.

https://www.marketingforgreatness.com/the-marketing-for-greatness-podcast/

Let's Get Social!

Official BIO	https://www.marketingforgreatness.com/jessicacampos/
Instagram	https://www.instagram.com/coachjessicacampos/
Facebook	https://www.facebook.com/marketingforgreatness/
Direct contact	https://www.marketingforgreatness.com/get-it-started/